A.S. A

P9-CPY-113

WE PROPHESY IN PART

WE PROPHESY IN PART

A Re-examination of the Liberty of Prophesying

◆❧ by ❧◆

WILLARD L. SPERRY
DEAN OF THE HARVARD DIVINITY SCHOOL

LYMAN BEECHER LECTURES
Delivered 1938, before the Yale Divinity School

HARPER & BROTHERS PUBLISHERS
NEW YORK   LONDON

PREFACE

SOME months ago I went into the study of
my former colleague, the late Professor Francis Greenwood Peabody, to ask him to share my
pleasure at the honor which Yale had done me
in inviting me to give the Lyman Beecher Lectures for the coming year. He congratulated me
warmly, and then said with a touch of genial
malice, "But what are you going to say? There
isn't anything left to say. Phillips Brooks said all
that can be said about preaching, and all that
needs to be said, in his lectures long ago." Professor Peabody need not have labored the point.
I was already painfully aware of my dilemma.

Sermons, however, are not preached to a mo-
tionless world. They are preached to men and
women who are on the march. When, as in our
time, that march is long and rapid and forced,
words which were pertinent yesterday lose their
pertinence today. Preaching is, for the man who
does it, a dual transaction which must reckon with
Christian truth on the one hand and with the
mind of the hearer on the other hand. Most of

us who have been preaching for some time will agree that technically it is mainly a task of finding the exact range. The successful preachers of any day—successful in the best sense of the word —are by no means its ablest scholars; they are men who succeed because they can match their understanding of religion in the abstract by a knowledge of human nature in the concrete. That means speaking to men and women living under particular circumstances at a given time in history.

The warrant for continuing indefinitely such a series of lectures as this lies not in the possibility of perfecting still further the theoretical rules for making sermons, but in the necessity of constantly shifting our aim in a deliberate attempt to find the range of a world which refuses to stand still. It is only on such grounds that, at this late date, another Lyman Beecher lecturer can with self-respect take his place in the succession.

In particular I wish to express to the Dean, the Faculty, and the members of Yale Divinity School, my appreciation of their generosity in opening to me this opportunity—one which any preacher must covet and which no preacher can ever hope fully to meet. I am bound closely to

Yale by many ties. I take this occasion to ac-
knowledge gratefully the most intimate of all
the ties of blood, that of father and son. My beloved and honored father, a Congregational minister before me, graduated from Yale College in
'69, and later came on to the Yale Divinity School.
I myself passed one of the most formative and
interesting years of my life, '07-'08, as a graduate student in the School. Yale has meant so
much in my family tradition, and in my own experience over the last thirty years, that I welcome
gladly the occasion which brings me to its Divinity School again to consider our common concerns at this particular hour of perplexity and
opportunity for the Christian Church. I give you
all, friends at Yale, my thanks.

WILLARD L. SPERRY

Cambridge, Massachusetts
March 5, 1938

CONTENTS

Preface   V

I. *The Austerity of Prophecy*   1

II. *The Prophet's Woe*   25

III. *The Christian Prophet*   53

IV. *The Edification of the Church* 80

V. *The Cult of Unconventionality* 104

VI. *Our Professional Skills* 134

VII. *The Timeliness of Our Sermons* 164

 The Lyman Beecher Lectures
  on Preaching   192

WE PROPHESY IN PART

CHAPTER I

The Austerity of Prophecy

THERE are in the Christian tradition certain phrases which echo down the years with authority. They were hammered out when the iron was hot. With the passage of time they have cooled into platitudes. But they are never forgotten, and in moments of historical insight, or of fellow-feeling for their authors, we can recover something of their original truthfulness.

In 1647 Jeremy Taylor wrote *A Discourse of the Liberty of Prophesying.** His discourse remains to this day one of the most Christian utterances of the stormy middle years of seventeenth century England. It is a compound of cool dispassionateness and warm charity. Long after its own day it is still read, while the bitter tracts of contemporary controversialists are forgotten.

The book owes its literary immortality, how-

* The Rev. Hensley Henson, D.D., then Rector of St. Margaret's, Westminster, and now Bishop of Durham, appealed to Jeremy Taylor's *Discourse* for the title of his Lyman Beecher Lectures delivered in 1909.

ever, not so much to its content as to the single happy phrase in its title—"the liberty of prophesying." For nearly three hundred years those four words have stirred the imagination of preachers. Every man who enters the ministry has heard them, and no man who has heard them is ever able to forget them. If the people to whom we preach might know that, whether they hear or whether they forbear, yet in our person there has been a prophet among them, we could enter the ministry with hope, continue it with courage, and end it with a good conscience. To be a freeman in this society of the world's unbought souls is an ideal we can never relinquish.

The task of perpetuating religion and of bringing it to perennial rebirth in history is committed to two men—the priest and the prophet. These two men appear at the dawn of every religion, or in the earliest hours of its day, and persist thereafter. In general the distinction between priest and prophet marks the contrast between Catholicism and Protestantism. The disunion of the Christian Churches is not, for the most part, a matter of traditional beliefs. There is, in spirit and substance, if not in verbal form, far more theological agreement among most churches than we commonly realize. The chief obstacle to church unity is met in rival conceptions of the church itself, and in particular of the ministry. These differences are not superficial. They go deep into our theory of the religious life, and they go back over many centuries to the beginnings of all religion. How does the minister of religion conceive his office, what does he think he is trying to do, what are his people expecting him to do?

For better or for worse, Protestantism has cast its lot with the prophetic type of religion. It is not for us, therefore, to criticize in too cavalier a manner the priestly conception of Christianity, which must have meanings and values we cannot fully grasp. Its survival, century after century, should convince us of the fact. We shall be more profitably employed if we try to improve upon our practice of prophesying. This is the act which is hereditary with us and native to us. The longer I live the more am I convinced that, while we should explore with sympathy forms of the religious life other than those which are second nature to us, we shall come nearest to the final truth and best serve the total cause by pressing forward along the way which is most familiar to us. We have one life to live and we cannot afford to waste it in a thin religious cosmopolitanism.

The words, "prophet" and "prophecy," are so

much a matter of mental second nature among us
that it requires conscious care to prevent their
use becoming also an abuse. As we grow older
most of us repent of the over-familiarity with
which we habitually refer to one or another of
the world's classics. On the strength of a bare
introduction to them we presume to a spiritual
intimacy with them which we do not have. We
complain in America, and complain justly, of the
wanton way in which lumbermen have stripped
our forests and farmers have desolated our soil.
Our priceless resources should have been more
carefully husbanded. Yet in the pioneer period
of his intellectual life every man of quick mind
is apt to go through the precious yields of the
human spirit in something of the same reckless
manner. It is only after we have discovered how
rare the true classic is, and what centuries of
racial experience, what years of personal discipline, have gone into its making, that we repent
of our too facile modes of knowing and appre-
ciating it. By the time we are thinking of dying
we begin to realize the worlds of unsuspected
truth and beauty which are still hidden from us
in the words, "Parthenon, Chartres, Hamlet, the
B Minor Mass," and what honest caution is needed
when we take these words upon our lips as repre-

senting in any way whatsoever realities with which we are personally identified.

From this peril religion is not immune; indeed, to this peril religion is peculiarly liable. Religion tells the story of the greatest lives that ever have been lived, and uses without reserve the most sacred terms in our human speech. The open Bible, supplemented by the open pages of Christian history and Christian devotion, spread before us without let or hindrance the best that words can do to give voice to the life of the soul. Saint Paul's speech before Agrippa comes to its end with the statement, "This thing was not done in a corner." The words ring true to the genius of Christianity. Our religion has always opposed the secret-society frame of mind, and has little in common with mystery religions, whether ancient or modern.

There is, however, no form of freedom which does not carry with it its peculiar perils, and the very candor of our religion has its attendant risks. Some thirty years ago Henry Churchill King wrote a book on *The Seeming Unreality of the Spiritual Life*. The title is both interesting and accurate. In so far as the Christian religion presents us day by day with what we call intellectual difficulties, President King's phrase intimates the nature of those difficulties. The spiritual life seldom seems to us wholly false, but too often it seems only imperfectly real. For modern men, their most grievous religious difficulties lie somewhere within this area. Our age is tormented with a sense, not of the utter wrongness of life, its flaming evil, but rather of its want of any major meaning and its grey futility. I am persuaded that this seeming unreality of the spiritual life is often due to premature identification of ourselves with the classical patterns of the Christian life, whether these patterns be persons, situations, or words. We are invited by the generous tempers of Christianity to become one with all such, yet any such "oneing of life"—to use an arbitrary word from mediaeval English mysticism—is a long process. The marriage of our meagre experience and of our very imperfect characters to the classical statements of religion is one which should be entered into "reverently, discreetly, advisedly, soberly." For neither Christianity, nor any other religion, can protect a man against the ultimate unreality which he invites by premature and reckless use of classical statements of the spiritual life as being the substance of his own personal history.

The general principle which we have been attempting to lay down has special pertinence when we return to our theme. The words, "prophet" and "prophecy," unless they are to be emptied of all meaning and reduced to the level of a commonplace professional tag, are among the most austere in the language. The liberty of prophesying, which we propose as our ideal in the ministry, is something more than the right to say what we happen to think at the moment in the bland trust that our words will be received as an inspired utterance. To vulgarize the term "prophet" is to destroy it altogether. So employed, it is little better than a kind of fiat paper money without backing either in the history of the past or the experience of the present.

The prophet first came to his religious maturity among the Jews. He spoke before he wrote, but when he began to write he had come of age. He was, to most of the Christian centuries prior to our own, an unknown figure. The sole interest which Christians took in him centered upon his Messianic predictions. We have now finally seen him as he was, a preacher to his own time. So well has the task of rehabilitating the Hebrew prophets been done that these men and their work, instead of being hidden from us, lie, if anything, too open under the garish light of day.

The problem which they present to us is quite other than the riddle they presented to the biblical scholars of the last century. So far from not knowing them, we know them, if anything, too well. We slip soon and easily into the habit of citing and identifying ourselves, as ministers of religion, with "the Hebrew prophets." But what do those three words mean? Unless they are to be deprived of all serious content they refer to some fifteen or twenty men who appeared in Israel over a period of five or six hundred years. There was, on the average, perhaps one prophet to a generation. When, as occasionally happened, two or three coincided in time, other generations went without their prophets.

If the analogy is to be accurately drawn, we are entitled therefore to look, during the first third of the twentieth century, for one or two men who perpetuate and reincarnate the original. Who would these men be? Gandhi perhaps; Wilson possibly; and Leo Tolstoi almost certainly. Yet each of these fails us at some crucial point. Gandhi has been too much involved in political strategy. Wilson, alas, seems to have lacked selflessness. The great Russian was too far above the battle. Persons at the left wing would nominate Lenin; but Lenin was not an original thinker, he was a scribe whose copy-book was filled with sample lines written by Karl Marx. There are minor prophets by the score and false prophets without number. The latter do not concern us. We hope to keep clear of the society of false prophets, and if we aspire to be true prophets we had best hitch our wagon to a star; it is the major prophets who have made history, not the minor prophets.

Protestantism is a type of religion which struggles for perspective. In the ceaseless endeavor to find the progressively more excellent way we must not level all values down and up. Once you have admitted the validity of a theory of relativity in such matters, you cannot demonstrate that which is more excellent without conceding that which, whatever its excellence, is less excellent. A uniform superlative destroys all distinctions and deprives our type of religion of its hierarchy of values.

I plead, then, in our thought and use of the words, "prophet" and "prophecy," for the majesty of their original meaning. My former colleague, Professor James Hardy Ropes, once remarked that he seldom used the word "prophet"; he saved it for great figures in religious history, and could not say that he had ever seen, heard, or known a prophet in the flesh. This is an extreme statement, yet of the two errors to which we are liable when dealing with the subject, his is preferable. We do well to set the standard too high rather than too low.

Let us look more closely, then, at that thin line of men whom we see passing in loose formation along the sky-line of Palestine from the eighth century B.C. What sort of persons were they?

They were a mature type. We are much too apt to think of the writing prophets of Israel as novel figures in history, unsired by any predecessors. Nothing could be farther from the fact. They were the product of a long process of trial and error. It is difficult, if not impossible, to estimate the degree of a great man's dependence upon the culture in which he appears. There is in him an unpredictable and irrational element. He is, to use a term from biology, a "sport," a radical departure from previous types and the possible parent of a new species. On the other hand, he seldom happens in history as a wholly independent and arbitrary event. He matures within a tradition, and from time to time flowers suddenly, full blown. You cannot say that the tradition has produced him, if in so saying you imply that the tradition has necessitated him, but you can say that apart from the tradition he is improbable, if not impossible.

The parallel of the Protestant Reformation holds here. We are too prone to think of the Reformers as new creations, novelties in history. We do so because we trace our ancestry direct to them, and are content to leave it there. Enough for us that we have Luther or Calvin for our father. But the church door at Wittenberg was not so much a point of departure as a point of arrival. The first quarter of the sixteenth century saw the resolution of issues which had been recognised for centuries and of differences which had been felt with increasing discomfort for generations. The Reformation was the last act of a long drama; what it was to require as a sequel was another matter, the promise of a new and different play.

So it is with the writing prophets of Israel. Specifically they are a new type, generically they are the mature expression of an older type. In them the wanton elements of soothsaying have been eliminated, the fanaticism of an early day has been disciplined, strong emotions have been brought to the heel of stronger ideas, reckless prediction has given place to a sober pronouncement of the principles of enduring righteousness, and—most important of all—prophecy has taken on its distinctive moral quality. As you read the stray references to earlier prophets, and watch dervishes becoming fortune-tellers, fortune-tellers becoming foretellers, foretellers becoming preachers to their own time, you see the institution of prophecy undergoing a process of progressive refinement. The pure gold of written prophecy in Israel was reached only after much dross had been smelted away. Amos was a point of departure and in some measure a figure historically without beginning of life or end of days. As a prophet he would have been the first to admit that he was unprophesiable. But he was even more truly a point of arrival. The previous three or four hundred years of prophecy did not ensure him, yet he would have been impossible without the experience of those centuries.

This estimate of the facts is not without its professional suggestion for us. A prophet is a well-trained man, not an untrained man. This training is in part an endowment of racial experience which comes to him as heredity. It is, also, conscious self-discipline. Amos had been to no school of the prophets. He had spent his life on the fringes of the desert. But if we leap to the conclusion that his days were passed in what Wordsworth calls "that majestic indolence so dear to native man," we shall be wrong. His book intimates very clearly his <u>alert vigilance</u> in the solitudes which surrounded Tekoa, and that most costly of all the processes of life, <u>intense meditation</u>.

I challenge you, therefore, to cite any major prophet in history who has come to pass independent of a religious tradition or culture, and whose utterances owe nothing to a long period of honest self-discipline on the part both of his predecessors and of himself. You will be hard put to it to find such a man. In so far as the prophets have been "come-outers" they have never left an existing formal religion until they have satisfied themselves that they have exhausted its possibilities. The trait of passionate impatience which we recognise in the authentic prophet is a slowly matured conviction rather than a momentary irritation or irradiation.

If the ancient fact provides food for modern reflection we shall conclude that prophecy, whatever it means, does not mean idleness and the deification of random reflections which occur to us when we are theologically fancy-free. Our chance of being prophets depends in the first instance upon a sober acceptance of the tradition in which we stand, and an earnest desire to fulfil it. Prophecy implies, ultimately, that mysterious margin which inspiration adds to honest craftsmanship.

> Oh, the little more, and how much it is!
> And the little less and what worlds away!

I doubt whether any man is ever inspired—be he poet, painter, musician, preacher—unless, in the terms of rigorous self-discipline, he has kept his human half of the spiritual compact implied in the very idea of inspiration.

Our next statement about the Hebrew prophets is more disquieting. They were, with the exception of Ezekiel, laymen rather than clergymen. The distinction is not wiped out if we say that the priest was the professional religionist and the prophet the unlicensed practitioner. Whatever is meant by the repeated references to "schools of the prophets" in Israel, we are to understand that some kind of loosely organized society existed in that name, with its techniques recognised and passed on from man to man. The authentic prophets dissociated themselves from the schools of the prophets as sharply as from the priests. The prophet was the plain man, attacking the vested interests of shrines, temples and professional soothsayers. One whole half of his burden was the anti-clericalism which is always working as a ferment when the times are unsettled and men's consciences uneasy over the existing order. The moral indignation of the fourteenth and fifteenth centuries, as we find it in *Piers Plowman*, was mainly a lay protest. Tolstoi's relentless rebuke of Russian Orthodoxy was a layman's indictment.

On this point Amos is unequivocal. He went out of his way to stress his non-professional status. "I was no prophet, neither was I a prophet's son: but I was an herdman, and a gatherer of sycomore fruit; and the Lord took me as I followed the flock." Nothing could be more explicit. There has been, to my mind, in American history thus far, one figure who above all others clearly merits the title of prophet and to whom it is not misapplied—Abraham Lincoln. He fulfils in certain interesting details many of the specific requirements of the type. It is true that Lincoln's greatest words were not aimed against churches. His burden was the prophet's profounder concern for the vindication of the righteousness of God in the history of a nation. But Lincoln was a layman through and through. He was not a clergyman, nor the son of a clergyman. He had no theological training. He was a dresser of logs on the frontier, and he was taken from a flat-boat. His

Second Inaugural Address is, in its substance and its spirit, more nearly like the words of Isaiah or Jeremiah than any other of our classical utterances. No Christian sermon preached on this soil quite matches it as pure prophecy. There is a noble dispassionateness before the immediate political issues of the time, and a passion for timeless righteousness, which we instantly identify as prophetic. When Lincoln says that "every drop of blood drawn with the lash shall be paid by another drawn with the sword," since "the judgments of the Lord are true and righteous altogether," he has the ring of the Old Testament at its best. We feel that what he says is eternally so, even though his words are to our hurt.

I venture to suggest that this first and most striking characteristic of the prophet, his lay status, raises at once a question as to the propriety of our taking the term over as a form of self-designation. The prophet is a person who is more apt to be outside our formal ministry than inside it. We are professional persons, working inside a church as part of its supposedly necessary machinery. We ought to be quite aware—none more so—of the defects of churches. We ought to be trying to reform them. But a saving sense of humor should persuade us that there is something rather incongruous in berating our congregations on Sunday for the "sickness of an acquisitive society" and asking our parish committee for a raise of salary on Monday. The question as to whether or not a man can do his best work for religion inside the church or outside it is a real one. I have never forgotten that at the conclusion of my own theological studies in Oxford, Canon Streeter, who was then my tutor, told me that I ought seriously to consider whether I might not serve the cause of religion better as a layman. Many men, passionately concerned for religion, have soberly concluded that their contribution to the total cause must be made apart from churches. We cannot challenge their good conscience or deny the probability that, in their own cases, they were right. William James would certainly have been less effective in behalf of religion had he been a bishop!

There are, on the other hand, some of us who finally conclude that our best work can be done inside the profession of the ministry. I have never been quite certain what this decision implies. Does it mean that we have made our peace with the fact that we are average men, not geniuses, and therefore unlikely to be prophets of a major dimension? Does it mean a renunciation of the stern duty of prophesying and a shirking of the pains to which

the prophet is liable? Every man must here answer
to his own conscience. Meanwhile the greater part
of the steady, productive work of the world is done
by men living together in organized societies, and
no man forfeits the chance to make two blades of
grass grow where one grew before by deciding that
his life-work shall be sought and found in one of
the stable professions and institutions of his time.
Indeed, under the conditions of modern labor,
whether his task be research or organization, it is
increasingly difficult for a man to do work, of which
the time can approve, outside such societies and in
want of their resources. No man, then, need feel
that he has bargained away his soul if, having
taken his own measure and defined the task he
wishes to do, he enters a profession like the ministry
and an institution like the church. On the whole
such a choice is morally more defensible than an
insistence upon the right to be a petulant and relatively ineffectual minor prophet at loggerheads
with the world as a whole.

Having made the choice, however, a man is
under bonds to play fair. He must not dissemble,
either in word or deed, before his fellows. I say
this because there is abroad today a strategy in
dealing with supposedly doomed institutions which
is known as "boring from within." You scuttle the

ship in which you have signed on as a member of the crew. You have, of course, taken the precaution to cut the lashing of a convenient lifeboat which will be available for your personal use when the vessel goes down under your feet. The higher morality of certain of the newer gospels countenances and even urges upon us the entire propriety of such conduct. A subtle sophistication will therefore suggest to the would-be modern prophet that he get ordained and bore from within. This revision of the prophet's method, so we are to gather, is a change of tactics required by the more highly organized life of the modern world.

We all know in the ministry moods of holy anger against the smugness, the inertia, the worldliness of organized religion, when nothing short of the destruction of the whole fabric can satisfy our ideal demand. The Church seems, in a homely phrase of John Masefield's, "too broke to mend." In such moments of captivity within the institution, we ask to be led to some place between the pillars of the temple. We want nothing better than to get our arms around those pillars and pull down the edifice upon all concerned. Such an act is at least honest, and is also sacrificial because suicidal. But you cannot deliberately destroy more than one church in this way and continue in the ministry.

If you successfully wreck one church, you are unlikely to be instantly invited to repeat the operation
on a second church. That sort of thing can be done
once, but not twice. You have only a single career
with which to commit professional suicide. This
desperate remedy is not to be confused with "boring
from within," since the man-with-the-augur in
modern society always has a prominent place re-
served for himself in the Utopia which is to ensue.

The objection to attempting to be modern
prophets by boring at the church from within rests
upon its essential dishonesty. You are living a
double life, secretly destroying the institution which
ostensibly you are serving, and the whole transaction belongs to the area of espionage. Our world,
much less our church, will not be saved by spies
whose history is a living lie. You can respect any
hero who is in the open. You cannot respect and
you certainly will never trust the man whose conduct over many years turns out to be a studied
falsehood. We must heed the instinctive moral
judgment which tells us that, whatever other social
orders may be so achieved, the Kingdom of God
will not be brought to pass by such methods. Few
of us enter the ministry with a dual personality
and a conscious duplicity of purpose. Yet we are
at times tempted to play with this modern tech-

nique as necessary and salutary. The temptation is to be resisted. It is like a sunken ledge lying off the entrance to some harbor, where a whistling buoy moans its warnings and an occasional sea piles up and crashes in a thunder of foam—a menace to be given a wide berth if you wish to drop anchor in your desired haven. In short, the man who, with full knowledge of what he is doing, seeks and takes a place in an institution, is under bonds to act in good faith. He may earnestly seek its reformation and advancement by all constitutional means. He may not lead a double life. This is nothing more than a matter of common honesty, but at least it is nothing less.

I cannot attempt to resolve the riddle which I have proposed, how a professional churchman is to perpetuate in its classical form a religious type which has always been at its characteristic best a thing of lay status. The real problem is the initial one, whether a man knows himself to be of such dimensions that both the ministry and the church are too cramped for him. In that case he "can do no other." He must go his solitary way. Let it merely be pointed out in passing, that a refusal to be ordained or to have anything to do with churches is not, as many emancipated persons seem to assume, the automatic guarantee of a life of prophetic dimensions.

Our emphasis upon the prophet's lay status needs, however, careful interpretation. In one of his novels Mark Rutherford says of its hero that he was, happily for him, a lay person committed to no system or church. We shall be greatly in error if we think of the prophet, in distinction from the priest, as an uncommitted person. His commitments are more binding than those of any other person in the religious scene. It is true that he is not under bonds to ecclesiasticism, but he is not thereby quit of accountability to some external sanction and seat of authority.

The prophet is under bonds to God. His authority derives from God and his reckonings are made to God. His freedom is, therefore, more rigidly conditioned than that of any other of his fellows. Such freedom as he has falls within the familiar phrase of the Prayer Book, "whose service is perfect freedom." Those words consciously play with paradox and it is a fair question whether, in the vulgar sense of the term, freedom exists under such conditions. There is, rather, a "blessed necessity." This necessity may well be more satisfying to the human spirit than any enjoyment of unfettered private liberty. It is not, however, what men commonly mean when they speak of freedom.

In our attempt to reincarnate the prophetic pattern we are liable to fall into the error of scaling down our demands upon ourselves, rather than scaling them up. We can see that the gods of the market place are not sufficient seats of authority, and the lawless animal which survives in each one of us enjoys playing the iconoclast. Cromwell's soldiers irreparably destroyed a wealth of Christian art in the churches of England and, whatever our theological view, we find it hard to forgive them; but they must have had a thoroughly good time smashing things. Any man can have equally good sport today smashing the formal conventions of religion. He may even hallow his natural enjoyment by persuading himself that he thereby does God a prophet's service. He gets, temporarily at least, a feeling of emancipation and a sense of an enlargement of his nature and its powers.

The danger is, however, that initial irreverence toward lesser authorities may unconsciously crystallize in a man's character, so that he becomes incapable of reverence toward a higher authority. The pathway of deliberate irreverence is one which, on occasion, may be necessary. It seems sometimes the only plain way out of a moral and spiritual impasse. But conscious irreverence does not provide permanent direction for the prophetic life. A prophet should be a man who is more reverent than his conventional fellow-religionists. He asks more of himself, because he is accountable to a more exacting tribunal. In our reflective moments we all realize that the appeal from ecclesiasticism to prophecy must be an appeal from a lower to a higher court. If, therefore, we intend to make the appeal we must be prepared to take the consequences. We need no longer fear what man can do to us, precisely because we have the fear of God in our hearts.

CHAPTER II

The Prophet's Woe

"THE Lord God hath spoken, who can but prophesy?" This familiar question sounds the theme of all prophetic utterances, and gives us the one criterion above all others by which prophecy may be identified.

The Old Testament uses with the utmost candor metaphors drawn for the service of the religious idea from the experiences of sex. Some of them go farther than the proprieties of a later day would suggest. And all of them, perhaps, are open to the perils which attend erotic symbolism in religion. There is, however, sober occasion for their use. Chesterton says, somewhere, that the signs and the language of sex which we see scrawled as profanities on walls, are not without their warrant, for sex is one of the two or three elemental facts of life, and men swear only by that which they feel to be true. The imperious fact of sex was used by the prophets earnestly, not profanely. They succeeded, by the aid of this symbolism, in saying some things which it would be difficult to say with equal force in other words.

Consider, for example, Jeremiah's account of his call, or his recall, to his mission. The King James version shrank from the vigor of the original and decently veiled the metaphor which the prophet himself used. It substituted the English word "deceive" for the Hebrew word "seduce."

> O Lord, thou hast seduced me, and I was seduced: thou art stronger than I, and hast prevailed. . . .
>
> Then I said, I will not make mention of him, nor speak any more in his name. But his word was in my heart as a burning fire shut up in my bones, and I was weary with forbearing, and I could not stay.

It would be difficult to find any figurative description of prophecy more powerful and more accurate than this. The prophet never has an itch to talk, or to hear himself talking. The things he must say are in the main so unwelcome that his personal comfort would always counsel silence. The pages of his writings abound with witnesses to the fact. He pleads his youth, his ignorance, his inexperience, and, after the event, his failures.

But God—the "Hound of Heaven"—is "a tremendous lover, who follows, follows after." The prophet's excuses and evasions and flight are of no avail. He is overtaken and his resistance is overborne by the divine aggression. However strong he may be, God is stronger. His defences are broken down and he is "seduced." The conception of prophecy anticipates the final moment when he "shall see of the travail of his soul, and shall be satisfied." There is, for him, no other peace, no lesser satisfaction. The imagery is bold, but it has this advantage—there is no mistaking its meaning.

We have in these metaphors our first test for the prophetic experience. The things which we can quite as easily leave unsaid are no part of a prophecy. Every truly prophetic utterance has the quality of being forced upon a man, and then wrung out of him. This canon puts out of bounds most of our measured and more reflective utterances. Much patient and honest thinking may be done in want of the divine compulsion, but we create confusion of ideas when we identify words of which we are the masters with words which master us.

No man goes through a lifetime's ministry without some intimation of the prophet's woe. He may be self-deceived; nevertheless for him the necessity will from time to time obtain. He has no option but to yield to its imperious seduction. To do otherwise would be to harbor the lie in the soul, and to sin against the Holy Spirit. I should say, at this distance from the classical Hebrew pattern, that the chance that you and I might understand from afar off the experience of those great souls depends upon our knowing moments in which we have no alternative but to speak out, whatever the consequences. Certainly no man who drafts a sermon outline in his study after weighing the pros and cons of his arguments and choosing accordingly with discreet reference to the particular situation he faces, can regard the delivery of the resultant discourse as prophesying. It may be witnessing, it may be pleading as with a jury, it may be teaching, it may be exhorting; it is not prophecy. But if, in the presence of some situation which seems wholly wrong, there wells up in him an elemental indignation which he cannot suppress and a passion for the right he cannot curb, he has an intimation, at least, of what the authentic prophet is and does. This righteous indignation is not to be confused with political and ecclesiastical bad temper, or habitual fault-finding with the social order. I can say that only twice in a preaching ministry of thirty years have I been on the fringes of the experience. I doubt if any man comes within its range more than a dozen times in his life. For once the burden and the woe cease to be acute and become chronic, they lose their prophetic quality. It cannot be a

mere accident that there is a disparity in bulk between the recorded words of the historic prophets
of Israel and the collected sermons of the popular
modern preacher. The two things are different in
kind.

The Lyman Beecher Lectures are supposed to
deal with homiletics; and homiletics, according
to the dictionary, is "the art of preaching." Notice
that the dictionary does not say "the science of
preaching." The definition is significant because it
concedes that the preacher, like all artists, is a man
whose best work is inspired. Therein lies its element
of necessity. The ultimate source of inspiration and
the precise nature of the transaction by which a
man gets the divine fire from heaven are beyond
our understanding. Even though we do not profess to explain it, we dare not deny it. At an oral
examination in Harvard Divinity School some
years ago Professor George Foot Moore asked
the candidate, "Where did the Hebrew prophets
get the 'word of the Lord' which they spoke? What
had happened to them to make them use that
formula?" The student countered with another
question, "Where did Beethoven get the Ninth
Symphony? If you will tell me this, I will answer
your question." "Quite right," said Professor

Moore, "if we knew that, we should know all mystery."

The inviolate secret of the sermon must always be defended against prose explanations and still more prosy rules. <u>Every man's best sermons have the mysterious quality of being given to him</u>. Psychology can carry us much farther back than any prior method of analysis has yet carried us, over a chain of causation which reaches into the unconscious—reviving old, far-off, forgotten impressions and releasing them for present use. But the believer in God will never give up the conviction that the utterance of a prophet draws upon still deeper sources. The true origin of prophecy is

> The hold that falls not when the town is got,
> The heart's heart whose immured plot
> Hath keys yourself keep not.

> Its keys are at the cincture hung of God;
> Its gates are trepidant to His nod;
> By Him its floors are trod.

Inspiration cannot be communicated from one generation to another by any manipulation of factors known, or likely to be known, to the science of eugenics. You cannot breed a prophet; he happens. Inspiration may be studied, but can never be domesticated in the curriculum of a university. You can-

not instruct a man how to become a prophet.
Inspiration cannot be self-generated by rubbing the
dry sticks of hard study one against another.
Prophets are not the product of imitation, or auto-
suggestion, or requirements for a Ph.D. We ignore
at our own risk the conviction of all creative
geniuses that their power comes to them direct
from the spiritual order. Their claim must always
be inexplicable, and we had best be reconciled to
our agnosticism as to the precise nature of the
transaction.

One of the final words on inspiration—whether
poetic or prophetic—has been said by Francis
Thompson,

> Thou canst foreshape thy word;
> The poet is not lord
> Of the next syllable may come
> With the returning pendulum;
>
> .   .   .   .   .
>
> Vision will mate him not by law and vow.

We may hope for our best sermons that they will
approach the borders of prophecy, that they may
stand in some outer court of its sanctuary. We shall,
however, do our task as preachers a grave disservice
if we bracket under that caption everything we say
from a pulpit. No one knows better than the
conscientious minister how bleak the day is when

no wind of the spirit blows over the parched desert of his platitudes, or no breath from beyond stirs the dry bones of his sermon outline. "Behold there were very many, and they were very dry!" How often have we looked at the draft of a sermon, or even at the finished thing, and said "Can these bones live? O Lord God, thou knowest."

When the authentic experience comes, or such approximations to it as are our lot, life has few rewards for us that are more satisfying. To see things clear and clean and simply; to speak out of such vision, with feelings that are tugging at the leash; to be persuaded that some eternal scheme of things stands behind our words to warrant and to redeem them; all this is profound joy. God send that we be not denied it.

Yet no man who has ever thought and felt and spoken thus is rid thereafter of the danger which follows in the wake of words so uttered. The prophetic experience is apparently like the mystical experience of which Saint Bernard says that he who has drunk of this well thirsts forever after to drink of it once more. It is all that pleasure promises to be and is not. It is the gratification of the will-to-power in its most sublimated form. If we have ever known it, we want to know it again.

Phillips Brooks has said that he who lacks emotion lacks expression, and it is true that the utterances of the prophet are shot through with feeling. If a man's feelings are quick there is no graver moral peril for him in the ministry than the temptation to tamper with them in the hope that he may thereby bring on the prophetic moment. Likewise there is no vice, to which our profession is liable, more disintegrating than the deliberate attempt to put feeling into words that have taken form without feeling. The simulated thing betrays itself instantly to the hearer and recoils upon the doer. Of every such practice John Tauler said with brutal candor, "It shall be counted to a man for spiritual unchastity."

I suppose this is what Dr. Jacks meant when he once said that "a popular pulpit is a dangerous place for a man's soul." It is dangerous because no man who lacks strong feelings ever gets there. But emotional energy creates for the man who possesses it its own moral problems. If we aspire to be prophets there is no duty laid on us more exacting than that which requires us to distinguish between genuine emotion and its counterfeit, sentimentality. Emotion comes of its own accord, in its own times and seasons. We cannot induce it in advance, we cannot control it in transit, we cannot recall it when it is gone. It breaks over us like a great wave and throws us ahead of its onrush.

The counterfeit thing is what we know as sentimentality, and sentimentality is feeling which we generate for ourselves by deliberately tampering with our inner life. George Meredith was not wide of the mark when he described it as "fiddling harmonics on the strings of sensualism." The more I listen to men preach the graver this vice seems to me to be. We can forgive men their theological errors. We cannot forgive them the chronic unchastity of sentimental sermons. Try as you may, you cannot force into your words more feeling than has produced them. You can clarify your thought by criticism, you can improve the order of your words by correction, but you cannot put genuine emotion into either words or thoughts unless they have been emotionally conceived in the first instance.

Of all the phases of our life, that of feeling is the most lawless and incalculable. It keeps its mysterious secret to itself. "The wind bloweth where it listeth, and thou hearest the sound thereof, but canst not tell whence it cometh, and whither it goeth." There has been little said of inspiration and its resultant joy truer than those words of the Fourth Gospel. We do well not to cast out our psychological "nets to catch the wind." We had best let it blow when it will, and where it will, and as it will. Our part in the transaction is an intellectual and moral preparation of character for the hour when the wind gathers.

A man who would prophesy must, therefore, leave his feelings alone. They will keep their integrity only as they are not meddled with. He must try to find the truth and to discover the right. If he is successful in these quests, emotion will attend both the seeking and the finding. He must take and trust what emotions come in the process, but in their absence he must not try to superinduce them. For the flogged-up feelings of a sentimentalist are not the convictions of a prophet.

I come, then, to one of the most distinctive aspects of our whole subject, the type of utterance required by the moral passion of prophecy. The prophets have never vexed themselves or their hearers with reflective theological distinctions. They have always addressed themselves to the conduct of life. Their criterion is righteousness rather than orthodoxy. We preachers of today, who are concerned for the course that history is now taking and is to take in the near future, are therefore more nearly in a prophetic relation to our profession than were our predecessors who devoted themselves primarily to correctness of religious doctrine. All that is meant by the social gospel has fortified the prophetic type of ministry. We are very unlikely, in the liberal churches, to suffer any inconveniences because of our theology. Our churches are theologically tolerant and if they are persuaded that a man has the heart of the matter in him, they will allow him a latitude which in other centuries would have meant excommunication, imprisonment, torture, and death. If we get into trouble and are martyred professionally, it will be because we stir up, either within our church or without, strong opposition to our accounts of applied Christianity. The sunken rocks on which we may well come to grief are the interpretations we give to industrial, economic, and political matters.

No man whose conscience lays it on him to speak unequivocally on these themes should be discouraged from so doing. Only a coward will leave them permanently alone. On the other hand, we may not leap to the conclusion that everything said on these matters from the pulpits of our day is necessarily prophetic. We ought to be clear what we are supposed to be doing and what we intend to say, when we preach on such subjects. I have no one social gospel above all others to commend to you. I am concerned with the premises of prophesying rather than with its detail.

Prophecy addresses itself to the concrete world at hand. There is nothing that men do which falls outside its jurisdiction. Their policies of state, their ways of holding land, making money, dividing gains, their sexual practices, their class divisions— all these are fit subjects for prophesying. The prophetic conception of life is the theocratic. Prophetism—to use Heiler's word—presupposes the kind of society which the church of the Middle Ages at its best envisaged, which Savonarola dreamed of for Florence, which Calvin attempted to establish in Geneva, which the Pilgrims proposed to found on these shores.

Now the whole weight of the prophet's words rests upon their claim to a moral and religious absoluteness. The prophet is not comparing one person with another or one group with another. He is referring all men and all societies to a divine standard and judging them by that standard. Prophecy wholly lacks the "nicely calculated less or more" which prompts pronouncements at a lower level. Prophecy is therefore deficient in specific instruction as to practical ways and means for the moral life. It shows you what you ought to be, but does not go on to tell you how you are to meet the requirements of moral duty. It is impersonal, non-partisan, and often immediately impracticable. The two major themes of prophecy are these: man's sins as they stand discovered by the righteousness of God, and the nature of the ideal society in which that righteousness will be realized.

Consider the dispassionateness of prophecy, its non-partisan spirit. The first two chapters of Amos are usually cited as one of the best examples of homiletical skill of which we have record. The prophet plays upon the antipathies of his hearers, rouses their indignation, gains their sympathy for his thesis, and then turns on them to make the direct application. This is not the only occasion in the Bible on which this strategy is followed. Nathan used it in his rebuke of David; Jesus invoked it in his dismissal of the accusers of the woman taken in adultery. It is, if you will, a recognized and legitimate method of getting a prophetic truth stated and driven home. Amos knew what he was doing, and did it deliberately. But surely there is in the text no suggestion that Damascus, Gaza, Tyre, Edom, Ammon, Moab, and Judah are mere stage properties or rhetorical devices. Unless you know that Amos is speaking to Israel there is little to choose between the indictments which he metes out with even hand to both his hearers and their neighbors. All have sinned and all alike come under common condemnation. There are no exemptions or special privileges, but neither is there rhetorical over-statement of a single case. The living men to whom Hebrew prophecy is addressed are never spared, but we feel all the while that they are the objects of a fair-mindedness which gives to even the most unsparing denunciation its austere validity. This refusal to give way to partisanship, either in praise or blame, appears in Lincoln's repeated suggestion that neither North nor South could surely identify itself with God, and that both probably fell far short of the divine demand. In Lincoln's universe there was always the chance that it might be God and the North against the South, chastened by the deeper suspicion that it might turn out to be God against both North and South. If so, there was little to choose between them, and they must be dealt with as of a kind. This profound suspicion gives to Lincoln's utterances about the Civil War their prophetic dispassionateness and their prophetic power.

Over against the divine indictment of mankind, as the word of the Lord spoken by the prophet, there were the glowing pictures of the Messianic order. The imagery used was that of familiar and well-loved life. There was never any attempt to describe a hypothetical Utopia which "eye hath not seen, nor ear heard, neither hath entered into the heart of man." In this respect the Biblical Utopias run true to the concreteness of Jewish thinking and the anthropomorphic trust of Judaism in the latent possibilities of the life we now live and know. The Messianic hope of both Testaments is therefore far more appealing, and indeed far more plausible, than the highly fanciful accounts of strange societies bearing no relation to any world we can recognize, which have been drafted by most other political dreamers. In the Messianic order the finer traits of the familiar actual world at hand are given universal validity and permanence. There is no effort to make you desire or hope for a life quite unlike your present life at its best. If you wish to usher in a modern Utopia you will do well to take a leaf out of the Messianic prophecies of the Jews. No man wants his present world made over out of all recognition, even though the change is planned for his good. You can enlist him in your reform or revolution only if you can assure him that the best he already knows will be permanently guaranteed him in your perfected society. Even Jesus himself ran true to the prophetic type in this vital matter. The hope that he held out, when he rose from the table on the last night, was of a day when again he should drink the fruit of the vine with his disciples in his Father's kingdom.

The use we make of the Messianic prophecies in preaching will depend largely upon the nature of our audience. Its imagery is so much a matter of our mental second nature that we do not realize how remote it is from the secular mind of this twentieth century. For us, the spirit is so contagious that it reanimates the letter. The letter, however, is not without its homiletical difficulties. The lion and the lamb lying down together are symbols of the resolution of this world's most native antipathies. Yet the validity of all such language lay for the ancient Israelite in its literal truthfulness. The words, for him, described facts which were to happen; they were not verbal symbols which he had invented.

We all have realistic moods in the pulpit, particularly if we are speaking to persons who know little or nothing of the Bible, when the use of this ancient imagery from a remote past seems to cloud rather than to clarify thought and speech. You will certainly reassure the farmer in the dusty crater of our middle west if you can convince him that in God's good time "the parched ground shall become a pool, and the thirsty land springs of waters"; but you will not contribute appreciably to the solution of a steel strike if you tell those concerned that "the sucking child shall play on the hole of the asp, and the weaned child shall put his hand on the cockatrice' den."

Precisely how the final transformation is to be brought about the prophet never tells us. And when, as on the rarest occasions, he attempts specific applications of his teaching by trying to establish a working connection between the ultimate ideal and immediate fact, he is peculiarly unconvincing. Witness the closing chapters of Ezekiel. The vision of the valley of dry bones is terrific. The picture of God's flock, gathered again by the Davidic shepherd in the good pasture on the high mountains of Israel —gathered out of all places where they have been scattered in the cloudy and dark day—is profoundly moving. But when we go on to read that in the restored temple the altar shall be twelve cubits long and twelve broad, and the settle fourteen cubits long, and that the oblation of oil shall be "the tenth part of a bath out of a cor, which is an homer of ten baths," we know that we are off prophetic ground altogether and over in the bailiwick of the priest. And yet the difficulty is that, if you are to have a temple and make offerings, someone must tend to these details. This, however, is not the prophet's business, whether the details be ecclesiastical, political, or economic.

The ethical teaching of Jesus has a quality of absoluteness. If it be the ethic of an interim, that ethic has already parted company with all prudential considerations, and with the prospect of immediate practicability. We feel this absoluteness in many of the moral utterances of Jesus, which are both dispassionate and devastating. To the concrete problem of the proper division of money, even a just division, Jesus had nothing to say. "Man, who made me a judge or a divider over you? . . . Take heed, beware of covetousness." The words are a highly unsatisfactory solution of a specific problem, but are characteristically prophetic. Indeed, the teaching of Jesus is not ethical at all, if by ethics we mean the formulation of modes of conduct which can be set to work at once; it is religious teaching of the purest prophetic type. All issues are brought into the presence of God, to be seen and settled *sub specie aeternitatis*. Both the indictments which are made and the hopes which are held out are dispassionate and universal. Therein lie their majesty and the secret of their power. To live, mindful of them, is at times almost an agony, yet such is their felt validity that we can never put them out of mind and forget them. They cease to mock us and remain to rebuke and to inspire us only as we realize that their affinities are with religion rather than morality. Professor Whitehead says of this "impracticable ethics of Christianity"— which he calls mankind's "most precious instrument of progress"—"A standard had now been created, expressed in concrete illustrations foolproof against perversions. This standard is a gauge by which to test the defects of human society. So long as the Galilean images are but the dreams of an unrealized world, so long must they spread the infection of an uneasy spirit."*

We are ready, then, for two or three dogmatic propositions about the nature of our sermons on political and economic subjects. The statements are offered in brief and blunt form. Like all dogmas they are oversimple, yet I think they throw some light on this most delicate and difficult matter.

If a sermon is to sound the prophetic note it must make statements which aspire to be absolute. You cannot descend from that arbitrary level to the lower ground of a comparison of degrees of moral excellence and retain the quality which makes prophecy what it is. The moment you begin comparing men, parties, classes, causes, states, you are

* *Adventures of Ideas*, Alfred North Whitehead. New York: The Macmillan Company, 1933, pp. 20-21.

off the rock on which prophecy rests. If, for example, you allow yourself in a sermon to become involved in explaining why Stalin is warranted in "liquidating" some thousands of his fellow Russians, while Hitler is not warranted in "purging" a much smaller number of his fellow Germans, you are not prophesying. The fact that you may personally think that there is more hope for the world in Communism than in Nazism, does not make your appraisal of the relative merits of their official murders a prophetic utterance.

So likewise when the preacher attempts to make relative pronouncements about money, as though they were prophetic utterances, he confuses the issues. A prophet cannot determine at what economic level the income tax shall begin to operate and how rapidly the surtax shall rise. The fairer distribution of the wealth of the world is a consummation devoutly to be desired. It is a perfectly proper theme for a sermon. But a sermon dealing with this subject in detail cannot be a prophetic utterance, and any attempt to make it so is instantly felt to be unwarranted. That, I think, is why the pews often have a real case against the pulpit. The pews are wrong in saying that we ministers ought not to talk about such subjects. But the pulpit is wrong in assuming that, because the man who stands there is theoretically vindicating the liberty of prophesying, his ideas about the redistribution of wealth have an authority and sanctity which do not attach to similar pronouncements in the columns of a newspaper or in any other frankly secular medium.

A man may try in the pulpit to inject into such discussions a spirit of sympathy and patience and charity which will help us to take the next step, and this is tremendously well worth doing. It is perhaps the best day-by-day contribution we can make to the situation. But pointing out to people the next step proposed by Christian common sense is not prophesying. We have no right to expect for words so uttered the silent deference which is felt to be the due of prophecy. The utterances of a prophet are absolute, and of their kind final. "I am in earnest— I will not equivocate—I will not excuse—I will not retreat a single inch—and I will be heard." That is the prophet speaking a century ago to the institution of human slavery. He knew one thing and one only, that slavery was wrong. He refused to be drawn into the kind of discussion which has occupied us ever since, as to whether it was fair to indict the slave-holders of Virginia for the sins committed by the slave-holders of Mississippi, or whether the lot of the negro in Virginia was not on the whole better before the Civil War than it has been since. William Lloyd Garrison would not have been interested in such questions, real as they are.

All discussion, therefore, as to the relative degrees of liberty, prosperity, comfort, education, which obtain among the peoples of communist, fascist, and democratic societies is beside the prophetic mark. No prophet was ever given the word of the Lord on matters of more or less. Prophecy demands all or nothing. Much, if not most, of our preaching on these themes has to be done by means of a gospel of relativity. But we should not expect our sermons so conceived and constructed to be given any more consideration than the weight of their argument and their Christian temper deserve. It is on this proper interpretation and discharge of our duty that the laity instinctively insist. So long as we tacitly or openly claim the deference due to a prophetic utterance for sermons which do not and cannot accord prophetic treatment to their themes, our people will criticize us and, I think, criticize us justly.

If, then, we aspire to prophesy, rather than to debate or discuss in even the most charitable temper, where are we to find the certainties which will give to our words the absolute quality which prophecy demands? These certainties take their rise in conscience and rest on the appeal to conscience. The Christian religion is still very far from being codified and concluded. This is as true of its ethical system as of its theology. Yet there have been from the first, and still are, certain tempers which the world instantly recognizes as being Christian. They are far from being generally accepted in theory and still farther from being realized in fact. Yet there they are—and when we see a deed prompted by any one of them, we instinctively say, "That was a Christian act." We have no complete list of such acts, and there is still much room for disagreement. The Roman Church calls all contraceptive practices unchristian; the Protestant Church is increasingly inclined to sanction them. We do not agree on this elemental matter which is to make or unmake the future of the race. I do not see, therefore, that you can attempt to prophesy on birth-control. We shall need many generations of conscientious Christian practice of birth-control before we shall have enough evidence to satisfy us of its effects on the bodies, the characters, the souls of men and women, and on the natures of their children.

But when Lincoln gave the southern cavalrymen back their horses for the spring plowing, when Father Damien went to Molokai, and when Edith

Cavell said "Patriotism is not enough"—we bow our heads to prophetic words and deeds. They have an absolute quality for all who profess and call themselves Christians. Prophetic sermons will identify and celebrate such facts in their finality, leaving them to work their own changes in the common mind. That is the way to spread what Whitehead calls "the infection of an uneasy conscience." The sum of such certainties, in so far as it can be added up out of the centuries, is the standing ground of the prophet. What people are to do about it, how they are to set about changing their ways and their world, has never been his major concern.

Ever since I can remember, I have been hearing sermons on the social gospel. Important as the subject is, sermons on this theme are no easier to remember than sermons on more abstruse matters; and, alas, most of those once-heard sermons on the social gospel have gone down the wind of forgetfulness. But there was one such sermon that I have never forgotten, and whenever I remember it I can always recover its imperious power. It was not a sermon preached in church at all. It was not a long sermon; it was in fact very short, a matter of seven words which were used to underwrite a picture that appeared on the title page of a number of "The

Survey" many years ago. It was preached during a bitterly cold winter, when unemployment was general and suffering correspondingly widespread. A newspaper photographer wandering around the East Side of New York in the earliest and darkest hours of a February morning happened upon three or four little children, clad in the thinnest rags, lying asleep on a sidewalk grating where they might catch what little heat escaped from the windows of an underground bake-shop. They were covered with a threadbare, tattered horse-blanket which they must have filched from some dump heap. And so he photographed them. The picture was printed on the front page of "The Survey" and under it these words only, "For so he giveth his beloved sleep." That is prophecy.

Let me close with a single example of my thesis regarding the absolute quality of the prophetic utterance. I think that the most sinister portent of our time is the renascence of cruelty. We need not bother our heads about those tenderhearted muddlers, Nero, Diocletian, and Decius. They were amateurs. Indeed, as a classical historian has recently said, there was left in the ancient world some vague suspicion that the persecuting spirit was a bird of ill-omen which would eventually come home to roost. He tells us that strangely, and for no good political reason which we can discover, both the Diocletian and the Decian persecutions flagged and petered out, as though the men who were charged with them were themselves afraid of the recoil of their weapon. There seems to have been an instinctive revolt against the entire procedure. The Greek tragedians knew well enough that the gods would punish insolence. The Roman official seems to have suspected that they would punish cruelty. He lacked conviction for his task. Would that the residual decency of the Roman might reassert itself today!

Personally I am not interested in the prospect of ultimate Utopias which are founded upon the premise of an immediate cruelty, because I do not think such foundations can be permanent. There is no general world war raging at the moment, but as the Wisdom of Solomon puts it, "in the great war of ignorance, those so great plagues called they peace." The deliberate, wholesale sanction of cruelty, which is gaining headway everywhere, is one of the reasons why this so-called period of peace is morally plague-ridden. A practical reformer may be prepared to justify or condone the resort to cruelty; a candid revolutionary will probably invoke it. But a prophet must sicken of the whole business. He must know that this spreading cruelty of modern man, whatever rags of political or economic apology it may gather to hide its naked horror is, as John Woolman said of slavery, "a dark gloominess hanging over the land." No truly prophetic soul can compromise with it. A Christian minister who extenuates its manifestations forfeits all claim to prophecy, whether those manifestations appear as the purging of Germany, the liquidation of Russia, the civilizing of Abyssinia, or the morbid sadism of the American crowd listening in at the execution of Hauptmann. This happens to be the one point in the modern world at which I feel something like the stirring of an absolute moral conviction. If you do not feel this particular ethical absolute as I feel it, you must have at some other point your own mounting prophetic conviction and indignation. We shall recognize the prophet's spirit at work in us by the absence of all desire to haggle about more or less in the relative degrees of things. For when we prophesy we get wholly out of the comparative moods of work-a-day life into another world where a distinction between shades of grey ceases to satisfy us because we are face to face with a blinding whiteness and a black darkness.

CHAPTER III

The Christian Prophet

THERE is an ungenerous phrase, I think it is Thomas Carlyle's, about "Hebrew old clothes." The words concern the Old Testament.

Disparagement of Judaism made its appearance in Christian circles as early as the second century, and has been revived in most of the following centuries. We may be grateful that it has never prevailed. The refusal of the church to follow the lead proposed by Marcion has preserved the continuity of our tradition as a whole, and has saved for us a very austere religious literature. It is now improbable that Christianity as a whole will ever renounce its origin in Judaism. Our insights into religion and our attempts to express it would be greatly impaired in want of classical statements which we have in the Old Testament.

As formal literature the Old Testament is far superior to the New Testament. The books of the two Testaments are not of a kind. Those of the earlier canon aspired to permanence, and the verbal form of many of their narrative passages must have been worn smooth by retelling long before they took written shape. The books of the later canon were mostly occasional in their composition and never anticipated their inclusion in a Bible. Given the eschatological dreams of the first Christians, it could not have been otherwise. There was no occasion to try to write books which should last, and literary perfection would have been a useless luxury belonging to a doomed world which was already passing away. We do our Christian half of the Bible no injustice when we admit that there is little or nothing in its writing to match the majesty of Deuteronomy or the artistry of Job. The nearest comparable approaches to formal literature in the New Testament are the Epistle to the Hebrews and the Gospel of John. The former was written by a man to whom the Old Testament models were second nature, and the latter by a man who knew that the world, so far from coming to a speedy end, was going on indefinitely, and who realized that in such a world there is a place for an enduring literature.

On the other hand, we are much nearer to the books of the New Testament than to those of the Old. Though only two centuries lie between the last of the books of the Old Testament and the first of the New, there is a modernity about much of the New Testament which is wanting in the Old. The narrative portions of the books of Samuel and Kings are said to set the standard for story-telling in all time. The economy of words, the rapid movement, the eye for concrete detail, are un-matched. But we do not feel that most of these things could have happened to us just as they are told, or perhaps we might say that if they were to happen we should not recount them in just that way. The Old Testament narratives are supremely well-told stories, rather than scrupulous chronicles of events, therefore they remain for us parables of life. Whereas Luke's account of the shipwreck in the book of Acts is not merely something we might have experienced, his way of telling it is also ours. Someone much wiser than myself might be able to explain the nature of this difference. Is the way in which things are said in Greek nearer to the way we say them in our later languages than the Hebrew ever could have been? However these things may be, I defy any man who reads a first and a second lesson in church to obliterate from his tone of voice the difference which we instinctively recognise be-tween the two Testaments. Indeed, the necessity of making a vocal distinction between them is in itself one excellent reason for having two lessons instead of one. They offer and require the necessary element of contrast within the service as a whole, in want of which it tends to lapse into a monotone.

With the opening page of the New Testament we stand on the threshold of the modern world. The newness of Christianity was sensed from the outset. When we compare the two Testaments we cannot say that the early Christians were self-deceived. The originality of Jesus was not a specious novelty. Christianity soon discovered, at first to its surprise, that it was something more than purified Judaism of the prophetic type, just as Christianity today is culturally something quite distinct from reformed Judaism. Liberal members of both religions would agree that, whatever be the mystery of his person, Jesus of Nazareth was, as an historical figure, a Hebrew prophet of the classical type. But this agreement does not do away with the distinction between the two faiths. Anyone who has shared in the attempt to find common ground for the synagogue and the church knows well enough how different they are. The accents and inflexions are not the same. The attempt of one to speak the dialect of the other is an effort and an affectation.

In particular the Christian Church, as it came to know itself accurately, realized that its fulfilment of Messianic expectation had taken forms which the prophets could not have anticipated. Its claim to be the true and only people of God, intended by God from the beginning of the world, is not ingenuous. This claim was elaborated by the Apologists of the second century as a tactical move; but however far they may have succeeded in convincing themselves, they do not convince us. Their argument was a piece of anti-Jewish strategy, rather than a spontaneous witness to Christian experience. Something unanticipated had happened, and there is little use, either then or now, trying to prove that the Christian Church had been from all eternity implict in Israel.

Consider, for example, the most indubitably modern book of the Bible, the First Epistle to the Corinthians. Here is a situation with which we are entirely familiar. This is the world in which we live and where we are at home, a world of imperfect human beings pledged to an absolute idealism, with all the resultant dilemmas. Many of the questions to which Saint Paul addresses himself in his letter persist today in their original form, and the remainder can be translated into their modern counterparts with a minimum of effort. We have the awkward problems of conduct which arise when conscience does not square with common social custom. Even the Corinthian Christians shrank from being queer. We have the riddles of sex, still stubborn and unsolved by any set of rules. There is the mystery of immortality—"with what body do they come?" And then we have the various practical matters which concern the organization and conduct of a church. Altogether the picture is that of a group of persons closely bound up in an intimate society, thinking of the things which we think about, and, what is more important, thinking about them in much the same way that we think. It is all so like ourselves. As Professor Lake once remarked in an address to a group of divinity students, "It must be a great comfort to any Christian minister today to realize that no matter how bad his parish may be, the one which Saint Paul had in Corinth was worse!"

Now if you look closely at this crowded and contentious world of the primitive church, you can espy the figure of the man of whom we have been speaking in the previous lectures, the prophet. But somehow he lacks the stature which he had in the Old Testament. A great man should be seen alone, not in the company of other men equally great. So with the primitive Christian prophet; he is not the dominating figure that his predecessor was in the eighth century B.C. He is already a "member of a firm." He jostles shoulders with apostles, evangelists, pastors, and teachers. He divides both his influence and his authority with deacons, presbyters, and bishops. His function remains, in theory, precisely what it always has been; but he is not the only person necessary for what Saint Paul calls the "edification of the church." The scene is a busy one, calling for more than one kind of spiritual craft, and there are workmen scattered through the rising structure doing many different things, each of which contributes to the whole.

The New Testament leaves us in no doubt as to the validity, even the necessity, of prophecy. Prophesying is one of the Christian gifts. In the hierarchy of spiritual endowments "greater is he that prophesieth than he that speaketh with tongues." Every Christian should "covet to prophesy," since "the testimony of Jesus is the spirit of prophecy." Nothing could be more unequivocal, and apparently the ancient prophet has made the transition successfully and is rehabilitated in the new society—given, as it were, by the ministry of Jesus and the ever-present Spirit of Christ, a new lease of life in history.

Yet there is a difference. Not merely is the prophet now one among a number of the ministers of religion, but his claim to inspiration is subjected to a scrutiny more searching than any to which his predecessors were liable. The ancient prophet was often found out in errors of fact. Things did not happen as he foretold. No one ever thought the worse of him on that account, and at this distance we do not accord him less honor because he was unable to do what no man has ever done, foretell the future. His refutation by the event remains merely as a warning to us not to rest the case for prophecy upon prediction.

In so far as the ancient prophet was repudiated by his contemporaries, their ground of distrust was the man's character, which failed to accord with his words. The percentage of failures seems to have been high. The authentic prophet was the exception, and the routine prophet far too likely to be a fanatic or a charlatan. The Old Testament abounds with denunciations of such men. "Priest and prophet have erred." "From prophet unto priest every one dealeth falsely." There is "a lying spirit in the prophets." "From prophets is profaneness gone forth." The prophets "have seen vain things" and "find no vision." They prophesy "falsely" and prophesy "lies." They prophesy "to the wind." They "divine for money." They are "prophets of deceit." They work with "untempered mortar." Such indictments, in their permutations and combinations, may be cited to the point of tedium. The end was inevitable: "There is no more any prophet." His place in the organized religious life of Judaism was taken by another man, the scribe, who construed his office in quite other terms.

It is not the least of the many significant achievements of primitive Christianity that it rehabilitated the discredited figure of the ancient Hebrew prophet. From that day to this, the ideal has never been relinquished. But, in bringing the prophet to life again, the Christian religion had to safeguard the type against the evils which at an earlier time had debased it. Unlike the Old Testament, the New Testament contains no wholesale denunciation of prophets. In place of denunciation there emerges an entirely new attitude, a certain advance scepticism. The prophet is no longer accepted on his own recognizance. The burden of proof is on him. He must make good his claim to be the spokesman of God, possessed or inspired by the Holy Spirit. His words are heard and laid on the table.

There is, therefore, in the New Testament, a much greater caution in the presence of the prophet than was the manner of the earlier time. The Christian prophet was not persecuted, or imprisoned, or killed—at least by his own kind. He was, however, kept at arm's length and compelled to produce satisfactory credentials. Some sort of objective verification, a convincing correspondence between the man's word and his character, or the consenting sober second thought of the community, was necessary. The injunction, "Believe not every spirit, but try the spirits whether they are of God: because many false prophets are gone out into the world," is written plain in the New Testament.

Not only did his audience scrutinize the prophet with greater care, the prophet scrutinized himself.[1] We cannot say that the New Testament shows the marks of radical self-distrust among the prophets of the first and second Christian generations. We can say that it does discover a resolute self-criticism, which is prompted by a sense of personal responsibility for the movement. There is nothing finer in Saint Paul's writings—finer as proof of the scrupulousness of his character—than his anxious care not to identify all of his private opinions with what he believed to be the word of the Lord. On certain

[1] On I Cor. 14:32—"The spirits of the prophets are subject to the prophets"—my attention has been called to two sentences of A. von Harnack, *Sitzungsberichte*, Berlin, 1919; 527, 529:

"Because the spirits of prophetically-minded souls belong to order rather than to confusion, they submit themselves to the controlling will of the prophets: the Apostle had this experience in every church. . . . The Christians knew well that the spirit of the prophets is subject to the prophets, that is to say, not one prophet to another, but the prophetic spirit to the prophet; the least among them had this experience, which rests upon a holy self-discipline."

matters he speaks with that tone of conviction which the deeply religious man will always have, and on such occasions his word is "the word of the Lord." But on many matters he speaks more tentatively, "by permission and not of commandment." This is a distinction—if you will, a sophistication—which does not appear in Hebrew prophecy. The ancient prophet was often overcome by a sense of inadequacy for his mission, but his self-distrust arose from an awareness of his youth, his inexperience, his obscurity. The task was too great for him. Being human, he shrank from a work which meant unpopularity, suffering, and possible failure. It is never easy to be a lone man against the world, even though you are a prophet. The Hebrew prophet, however, did not as a rule question the validity of his prophetic call or his prophetic burden.

With Saint Paul it was otherwise. His mind was filled with the fermenting stuff of Christian theology and Christian morals; a hundred unsolved problems pressed upon him for answer. Only a very scrupulous man would have taken the care which he took to distinguish between what he believed to be his inspired utterances and what he knew to be his personal opinions. Prudence would always counsel such a man not to stress this distinction, even if he were privately aware of it. For the purposes of propaganda it is more important to seem certain than to be certain, since it is, alas, the quality of dogmatic certitude which communicates itself, not the content. We should be grateful to Saint Paul that at the outset of Christian history he disciplined the ministry of the church in sincerity by his own example. Since then no Christian minister has been warranted in deifying his every private thought. To this day the occupant of the Fisherman's Chair is both allowed and required to make a distinction between his *ex cathedra* utterances and his occasional expressions of individual opinion. The two are not of the same order of religious magnitude.

The result has been a sense of imperfect security on the part of the Church in the presence of what professes to be prophecy, and on the prophet's own part a much more rigorous scrutiny of his visitations by that which he assumes to be the Holy Spirit. The issues thus raised became one of the major themes of mediaeval piety. The classical mysticism of the Middle Ages, as a spiritual discipline, was concerned above all else with two practical questions: how are we to conduct life in the periods of dryness and bitterness from which even the holiest soul is not exempt, and how are we to be certain that our heavenly visitant is Christ and not the devil in disguise? This latter problem is a pictorial statement of a stubborn scepticism as to the probability that we are inspired men, a scepticism already patent on the pages of the New Testament. The validation of our claim to inspiration remains to this day a necessity with which we are repeatedly confronted and for which, even at this late date, there is no adequate apparatus. How are we to know that, when a man says that he speaks for God, he is in fact doing so? More particularly, by what means can we satisfy ourselves that from time to time we are granted, presumably direct from God through his Spirit, certainties which have for us, and ought to have for others, a weight that we cannot attach to our personal opinion, no matter how wise we may be?

Few professional problems which concern us as ministers are more important than this. The pulpit is traditionally a place of authority. Its authority is derived from the experience of the man who stands in it, rather than from any delegated powers. Meanwhile the pews still wish to hear a man speak with that quality which we cannot describe otherwise than as authority. If in the pulpit we exceed our authority, and more particularly if we simulate an authority we do not possess, we are destroying confidence in ourselves and in the profession as a whole. Whenever we sin in this way we make it so much the harder for the authentic prophet. One of the soberest critics of the Protestant Church in contemporary America says that the decline of its influence is due to the growth of precisely this demagogy in its pulpits. Men invoke for their sermons the deference due to a truly prophetic utterance, when plainly they have not troubled even to master the facts upon which they are making their sweeping pronouncements, much less received any direct illumination from God. The spirit in which you and I enter a pulpit, and what we think we are to do when we get there, matters greatly for the future of preaching—and this means the future of our kind of church.

It is here that the Christian religion makes a definite contribution to the institution of prophecy. Christianity stressed, to the immediate detriment of prophecy, but to its ultimate good, the possibility of self-deception. "All deception" says the *Theologia Germanica*, "beginneth in self-deception." In one form or another that note is sounded in every searchingly Christian writing. So in 1650 Cromwell reminded the General Assembly of the Kirk of Scotland "I beseech you in the bowels of Christ think it possible you may be mistaken." "This above all," says the old monk in the *Brothers Karamazov*, "This above all, don't lie to yourself."

What, then, are the proofs that may be applied to our own more moving experiences which suggest a possible visitation of God's Spirit? Orthodox Protestant theology had for three centuries a simple answer to the question. Our moral feelings, motives, convictions, purposes are to be declared the prompting of the Holy Spirit if they are found to accord with the Bible. This was Calvin's thesis in the *Institutes*.[2] But Calvin's rule of thumb is not without its difficulties. There is a prior problem: How are we to know that the Scriptures themselves are inspired? To this question Calvin had his answer ready made—by the witness of the Holy Spirit. Calvin sees that he is caught in a vicious circle, half admits it and then dismisses the matter abruptly. Of all known methods for the verification of inspiration that proposed by traditional Protestant theology is the least satisfactory. We cannot deny Calvin's major premise, that the inspiration of the Bible is guaranteed by the witness of the Spirit of God within our own souls. Although

---

[2] *Institutes of the Christian Religion*, Book I, Ch. IX, 3. "For the Lord has so knit together the certainty of his word and his Spirit, that our minds are duly imbued with reverence for the word when the Spirit shining upon it enables us there to behold the face of God; and, on the other hand, we embrace the Spirit with no danger of delusion when we recognize him in his image, that is, in his word."

we no longer accord this guarantee indiscriminately to the Books of Judges, Ecclesiastes, and the Gospels, we are in general of Coleridge's mind when he said, "I know that the Bible is true because it finds me." We follow the logic of the process and trust the living Spirit within us to aid us in the task of a perpetual reinterpretation of Scripture. But we do not confine that Spirit to the letter of a book.

The truth is that no church respresenting orthodox Protestantism has ever succeeded in vesting final religious authority in a book, since no book is self-explanatory. Every book needs interpretation. Fundamentalism abides by the old dogma of a verbally inspired Bible, but can read into that Bible meanings which honest scholarship cannot read out of it. Fundamentalism enjoys therefore the theoretical advantage of having an external seat of authority by which the mobile Spirit of God in living men may be tested, and the practical advantage of a highly subjective interpretation of that authority. This paradox remains one of the major acts of unconscious self-deception in Christian history. So long as the deception is not identified the process can go on. Once a man becomes aware of it, the whole edifice comes down around him like the deacon's "one-hoss-shay."[3] There is, I think, no permanent hope for us in this direction. It does not suffice to turn the pages of your Bible to see whether you can run to earth proof-texts, or exemplars for yourself and your own immediate beliefs. If you are persistent enough, you can find anything you wish in the Bible. One remembers the story of the early English missionaries to New Zealand who translated the Bible into Maori for the benefit of their docile and pious converts. All went well until the Maoris were suddenly possessed by the conviction that they were the children of Israel and the English were the Amalekites, and proceeded accordingly!

In our Christian tradition the oldest, and to this day the most reliable, test of any man's claim to inspiration is a character which conforms to his words. The words of Jesus are definitive and final. "By their fruits ye shall know them."

There is in Phillips Brooks' *Essays and Addresses* a passage in defence of this criterion.

Every change of religious thought ought to justify itself by a deepened and extended morality . . . The manifestations of devoutness are variable and mistakable. The manifestations

---

[3] That poem was written as a thinly veiled caricature of the fortunes of New England Calvinism, which was to run smoothly until it went to pieces all at once.

of the moral life are in comparison with them invariable and clear. About my being humble and full of faith any man may be mistaken. About my being honest and pure it is far less possible to err. Therefore it is a blessed thing for all religions that the standards of morality stand clearly facing it and saying, "Can you do this? Can you make men brave instead of cowardly, kind instead of cruel, true instead of false?" For every new form of religious thinking it is a blessed thing that, full of its first fresh enthusiasm, it is compelled to pass along the road where the old solemn judges sit who have judged all the ages, the judges before whose searching gaze many an ardent young opinion has withered away and known its worthlessness, the judges who ask of every comer the same question, "Can you make men better men?" No conceit of spirituality or wisdom must make any new opinion think it can escape that test. He who leaves the plain road where the great judges sit, and thinks that he can get around behind them and come into the road again beyond where they are sitting, is sure to fall into some slough of subtlety and to be seen of men no more.[4]

The difficulty is, however, that such a test requires time. It takes a community years to know a man well enough to be convinced that his life gives weight to his words. It takes the man himself an equal length of time to distinguish between those of his ideas and words which, if not fully prophetic, approximate to prophecy, and those which fall short

[4] *Life and Letters of Phillips Brooks*, Alexander G. Allen. New York: E. P. Dutton and Company, 1900; Vol. II, p. 545.

of it. He arrives at the distinction in two ways. He finds that the emotion which attended thoughts and words of a prophetic kind can always be "recollected in tranquillity." Ideas of lesser worth cannot be heated again in the fires of feeling and the inference is plain: in so far as they were attended by ephemeral emotions they were sentimentalism. The substance of prophecy can always be deeply felt whenever the mind reverts to it. In the second place he observes that prophetic ideas have made a difference in his own character and conduct. Thoughts which pass through the mind and words which pass the lips leaving no change or consequence in life are patently no part of prophecy. This test, which Professor Hocking has happily called "a negative pragmatism," is one which we may trust.

Meanwhile this verification of the truly prophetic idea by subsequent tranquil recollection, or by its fruits in character, is a process which takes time; and this necessary time element introduces into any immediate situation a practical difficulty. Life is so organized that often we must act, either following some reputedly prophetic leader or turning away from him, without waiting to see what the fruits of his words are to be, whether in his own person or in their social consequence. Many of our judgments have to be made under the pressure of a hurried immediacy. What are we to do then?

At such times, if we are Christians, we shall appeal to Saint Paul's court of last resort—the common sense of the church. This is not society as a whole, it is the Christian community. There is little doubt that in spite of the glaring defects which attended its moral immaturity, the church at Corinth was bound together by devotion to an absolute ideal, and by a fervor of charity. And Saint Paul trusted the newly given grace of *Agape* more than he trusted prophecy itself. Given the presence of such charity he referred all claims to prophetic inspiration to the common sense of the church.

The Christian religion was then, and remains today, foolishness to those who do not accept its premises. But within its own four walls our religion has never professed to be the sum of the doings in a madhouse. It is one thing to allow a candidly unchristian man—unchristian both in his interpretation of the universe and in his ethical code—to call you a fool; it is another thing to admit to yourself that, given your Christian premises, you still are a fool, and to comfort the brethren with the reflection that we

are all fools together. Our religion, like every
other religion, has played with the theory that
the appeal to irrationality provides it with its
most powerful apologetic. *Credo quia absurdum
est,—credo quia impossibile est.* This amazing
statement makes its appearance early in the history
of Christian theology, and reappears constantly. It
is always a product of weariness and of sophistication. Tactically it gives to those who employ
it a strategic advantage in that it turns the edge
of every criticism brought against it. You cannot
argue with a man who tells you at the outset
that he has parted with his reason. From his
point of view he has put himself in an impreg-
nable position, and by capitalizing his intellectual
liabilities he has done away with that common
ground where thoughtful men may meet. Meanwhile, no man has ever explained the paradox
involved—namely, why a resort to deliberate irrationality is the one form of religious apologetic
above all others which has fascinated, and in a
measure also satisfied, the subtlest minds. It is
curious—is it not?—that the keenest thinking
of the world is so often devoted to demonstrating
the futility of all thought. This is as true within
Christian theology as in the general world of
philosophic speculation.

We can only say that the church as a whole has never sold its birthright, in the reasonable Word of God, to studied irrationalism. Simple, direct, and earnest thinking has always been of good report in the church. There is about Christianity at its best a sobriety of mind which anyone can recognize. Of the two errors to which we are liable—an over-intellectualism or a wilful irrationalism—the latter, bad as the former may be, is worse.

If it be said that the church has degenerated since its first days, that its common sense is today nothing but a pious transcript of the shrewdness of the kingdoms of this world, and that, therefore, there is no substantial body of Christian conviction left to which the prophet's claim to inspiration may be submitted, then such statements raise the question why it is worth while to live and work in churches at all. The Christian Church of the twentieth century, particularly the church which makes for itself "low" claims rather than "high," is simply ourselves, all of us, involved in the dusty and muddy and unideal world, gathered together in this particular relation around certain memories and purposes and hopes. The church is not all of our life, it is not as much of our life as it ought to be.

But it is at least part of our life, and my own persuasion is that, however imperfect churches may be, they represent the consciously better self in us, even though they still include within their walls other selves which ultimately will have to be laid aside if we are to become fully Christian. Any man who lives and works in churches has long ago ceased to idealize them in fact. But if it be true that the religious life is an attempt to achieve something like an accurate sense of perspective, then we have no right to forfeit, by wholesale denunciation, such hard-won achievements as are ours. People who go to church, whatever their defects may be, know that they are there faced with an absolute idealism. Churches, as institutions, are no worse than colleges or business corporations or labor unions. They only seem worse, because the principles around which they are supposedly organized are so much more exacting. It is the contrast between what we ought to be as Christians and what we are as churchmen which creates the permanent scandal of ecclesiasticism. I stand by my thesis, that it is the consciously better self of us which continues to go to church, not the self which is worse. Personally, in times of trouble or conflict, I would rather commend my case to any hundred professing Christians drawn by lot, than to a like number of persons drawn at random off the street outside. For there is, if not a powerful love at work in the church, at least a remembered tradition of catholic charity. The common sense of the Christian community is as reliable a guide to right and wrong as any secular common sense which may be had elsewhere. This may be saying very little, but we have no business in these days to wipe out a hard-won distinction in wholesale denunciations of the church and a guileless appeal to almost any other form of organized life in the modern world.

In the course of its report to the full session of the World Conference on Faith and Order, held at Edinburgh in 1937, the Section which dealt with "the Church of Christ and the Word of God" said that

All manifestations of the Spirit are manifestations of God's divine activity. It is here that prophecy finds its place in the Church's corporate life. . . . Every age has its own problems and its own difficulties, and it is the work of the Spirit in every age to apply the one truth revealed in Christ to the circumstances of the time. Moreover, as past experience shows, these new applications bring to the Church a new understanding of the truth on which they rest. The Spirit may speak by whomsoever He will. The call to bear witness to the Gospel and to declare God's will does not come to the ordained ministry alone; the Church greatly needs, and should both expect and encourage, the exercise of gifts of prophecy and teaching by laity, both men and women.

Certain of the continental churches, which find their sanctions in "the sole authority of Scripture," took fright at the suggestion that the laity should be "encouraged" to prophesy. The excesses of primitive Montanism and more recent Anabaptism seemed to linger in their memory as an occasion for caution. Their fears were quieted by the insertion of a statement, offered by a Quaker, that "the prophetic ministry is never safe without a corporate discipline." It was interesting to discover that the one Christian Church which rests its case solely upon the authority of the Inner Light is also the church which appeals most constantly to "the sense of the meeting" for objective verification of supposedly prophetic utterances.

Whether or not at this late date we are warranted in testing all claims to prophecy, our own included, by the common sense of the Christian community, I leave for you to decide. If you are not willing to do so, your unwillingness raises the question whether the ministry is the place where you can most effectively serve the cause of religion.

Meanwhile Saint Paul was right in saying that in the hierarchy of Christian gifts and graces prophecy no longer stands in lonely eminence. It is one among other of the ways in which God reveals himself to man. Greater than the would-be certainties and dubious infallibilities of prophecy are the deeper tempers which we know as faith and hope and charity. It is less important, for the Christian ministry, that you speak infallibly from your pulpit than that you know what it is to believe, and to hope, and to love. In Christianity it is no longer enough to tell the truth. Brutal truth-tellers may have sufficed another day, but given the Christian religion the truth must be spoken in love. The mental temper which attends that love is, in our religion, as in the world of our mature human affections, an irradiated common sense, a feeling for actuality, an unwillingness to sacrifice the sober and precious realities of life to romantic illusion. The common sense of Christians is not a shop-soiled and marked-down idealism; it is their part in a total thoughtfulness of things which is shot through with *Agape*.

For these reasons, therefore, our private claims to prophecy can never safely dispense with the confirmation which is had from the Christian community, as it cannot hope to escape from the criticism and correction of the community. The gift of prophecy is recognized as part of our endowment as Christians, but its exercise is conditioned by our prior obligation to be men of faith and hope and charity. Hence, even at our prophetic best, we shall only "prophesy in part."

CHAPTER IV

The Edification of the Church

AMERICA is a land of hundreds of denominations and thousands of churches; yet there is no country in Christendom where a feeling for the Holy Church Universal is less strong. We have no single established church, and in the want of any such dominant body our sense of the church is diffuse because democratic.

Denominationalism is our method and our mental habit. The "denomination" is so much a thing of second nature with us that we seldom realize how distinctive it is of American life. Strictly speaking, there is no such thing as sectarianism in this country, for the idea of the sect implies separation from some church which occupies a position of prestige and power. Such words as "dissent" and "nonconformity" have no pertinence on our shores. The conventional pattern in Europe is that of a single dominant body which, by past history or present political status, is the traditional church of the whole peo-

ple. From this parent church <u>dissenting minori-</u>
<u>ties split off to feed the soul thereafter upon</u>
<u>actual or imagined grievances</u>. This setting of
the scene has no parallel among us.

American life has been predominantly individualistic. Its pioneering has been done by solitary adventurers. Its highest prizes are still open
to those who were born in simplest circumstance.
Its family fortunes have been built up by re-
sourceful speculators. When America thinks of
Europe, it remembers with glee the cleverness
of its Connecticut Yankee in King Arthur's Court.
Its daily news is a matter of vivid personali-
ties rather than general social trends. Ours is
a land which has encouraged every man to take
himself seriously, and to make the most of himself; his native inclination to do so has for a
hundred and fifty years been dignified as an in-
alienable right, and is seldom censored by a
sober measure of his own powers.

Our cultural individualism is reflected in the
life of our churches. American institutions, at
the time of the Revolution, drew more freely
upon the life of New England than upon that
of any of the other colonies. Therefore "the
New England Way" marked the subsequent
church life of the country. Congregationalism was

the original form of the Christian Church in Massachusetts; it became the dominating type during the Colonial period and has remained the norm until this day. I do not mean that at this late date Congregationalism occupies a position of peculiar preeminence, but rather that the polity which it shares with other churches similarly organized has been the natural transcript of American culture. Its polity has communicated itself in practice to churches which in theory are organized upon quite other principles. Dr. Arthur Headlam, the Bishop of Gloucester, has more than once said that from the standpoint of England—and of Europe in general—"all American churches are Congregational."

This fact—and I take the fact to be incontrovertible—has done much to determine our conception of the Christian ministry, in that it has given a larger place to the prophet than to the priest. The priest is a person whose offices are impersonal; any attempt to individualize the ministry of the priest cuts at the very conception of priesthood; he is the voice of all sorts and conditions of men. The prophet, on the other hand, is never impersonal; the more sharply cut his features and the more striking his individuality, the more effective he is likely to be. Not merely self-knowledge and self-discipline, but self-expression and self-assertion as well, are necessary to his ministry. The total thrust of American life encourages the would-be prophet to stir up whatever preaching gifts he may have. Preaching has been taken seriously in America, and our roster of successful preachers over the last hundred years is as distinguished as that of any other Christian land. We have, therefore, an individualism in church life expressing itself naturally through the preacher, whose work in turn confirms the already atomistic type of church which has made him what he is.

It is only when you happen to find yourself in some quite different environment that you begin to see the American church and its ministry in perspective. Axioms which are generally accepted on this soil have no meaning elsewhere, or, if a meaning is conceded, it is challenged. Sermon methods and a sermon style, which would be instantly understood here, create perplexity or even cause scandal yonder. The American preacher abroad may have an interesting experience; he will, however, find it almost impossible to speak directly to the minds and hearts of a congregation. There is no country to which we are more intimately bound than England, and yet any sensitive American preaching in England must be aware of a difference. That difference I should attribute, not to any wide divergence upon matters of Christian faith and practice, but to the tempers of church life in England as represented by the contrast between the Establishment and Nonconformity. This is the background before which sermons are preached in England, and we are entirely without that background. We do well, therefore, to realize that the normal Sunday morning service in an American church is by no means a universal pattern; it is distinctive of America, if indeed it is not peculiar to America.

The American preacher, standing in the prophetic tradition and finding his instinct for prophecy reinforced by three hundred years of individualism, has always spoken directly to the workaday life of his people. Like his prophetic predecessors, he has been an intermeddler in their worldly affairs. The gulf between the sacred and the secular is not nearly so wide or deep here as it is in older countries. The peculiar prestige of the church in an old society is derived from a suggestion of aloofness; it is the house of a God who approaches the "wholly other."

Our church life is intimate and informal; the congregation and the parish are a community of friends: good comradeship is a recognized part of our creed. The week-days of a well organized parish are filled with opportunities for "getting together" under the roof of the church, or in the interests of the church. The very fact of being "together" under such auspices is itself counted one of the natural expressions of the Christian life. Who shall say that we are not right?

This failure to observe the distinction between Sunday and week-days, between things sacred and things secular, has laid the American church open to the charges of vulgarity and worldliness so often brought against it. The average American Protestant Church is said to be the docile maid-of-all-work in a bourgeois household, the slave of the God-of-things-as-they-are, helpless to change them and too timid to rebuke them. No one, I think, will deny the identification of the average American Protestant Church with the "middleclass" mind and morals of its people. This, we were once told, was its strength; this, we are now told, is its weakness. Only as it can succeed in breaking the bonds which enslave it to a craven conservatism can it hope to save its people from their sins.

I do not deny the elements of truth that have provoked this indictment of the church life with which we are most familiar. It may be worth while, however, to suggest that there are certain elements of strength and hope in our situation. A church which is so aloof from the life of its people that it fails to impinge constantly upon their intimate daily affairs, is in grave danger of losing its hold over them. One hears everywhere in Europe gloomy statements about the decline and decay of the church. It is hard to estimate the precise measure of truth in these statements, and yet one gets the impression of great institutions which are too detached from common life and secular interests. Why did the Russian Church, so far as the vast majority of its communicants were concerned, crumple up so completely before the aggression of atheistic communism? No one has ever questioned the beauty of Russian liturgy; no one has ever denied the piety of Russian mysticism. Nevertheless, when the storm broke, the rank and file of the Russian Orthodox Church membership seems to have been unable to withstand it. Perhaps it is impossible for an alien to appraise that tragedy. At this distance, however, one cannot resist the conclusion that the collapse of the Russian Church was due in part to its failure to keep its thought abreast of the times. Eastern Orthodoxy has always rejoiced that its doctrine has remained substantially unmodified since the ninth century, and a good many centuries have elapsed since that day. The gulf between the theological mind and the lay mind had become so wide that the span of the bridge across it collapsed. The Roman Church, by contrast, has always had an adequate apparatus for the interpretation of its deposit of primitive faith and for the ethical application of its beliefs to ever-changing circumstances. Rome does not move impetuously, but Rome has never failed to move with the ongoing centuries.

If there be a collapse of the church in sight in European countries other than Russia, I suggest that this collapse, when it comes, will be due in part to the too great aloofness of old and aristocratic churches from the contemporary concerns of plain people. In countries where the Christian mind is still active, and the Christian conscience still vigorous, attempts are being made to identify churches more intimately with the life of the people. But how to turn a mediaeval cathedral to religious account in the midst of a modern industrial society is a riddle not easy to read.

We have no such problem in America. Our people, for better or for worse, are familiar with a religion which speaks bluntly to their homes, their offices, their workshops. They may not always like what it has to say, and they do not always reform their ways in consequence; they are, however, thoroughly habituated to prophetism. Now no prophet can come down from the mountain, where he gets his solitary inspiration, to the dusty level of common life, without running the risk of being soiled thereby. Perhaps the difference between a true prophet and a false prophet is this—that the false prophet is not aware of the "stain and slow contagion of the world," while the true prophet is vividly alive to that peril and is constantly struggling to recover for himself and for the world the purity of his vision. Be this as it may, we do not have to reckon in America with a church which is so aloof from the daily lives of our people that it is in danger of ceasing to have anything whatsoever to say about their daily bread—the way it may be earned and the way it should be eaten. I should expect, in case of genuine spiritual crisis, to find in this country a Christian resistance to aggressive atheism or candid materialism more stubborn than we now anticipate.

The religion of the average American is not an "opiate." He has heard from the pulpit by this time far too many challenging restatements of his culture to suppose that no change is in store for him. He is mentally ready for a different mode of life if need be, even though the slothful human animal in him may not welcome it with enthusiasm.

The alternative to a prophetism, which must be always more or less muddied by the unideal world in which it lives and works, is a mystical detachment which is to be had only at the price of social ineffectuality. You cannot have it both ways. Harnack, in his essay on Monasticism, points out that centuries ago the Eastern and Western Churches came, in this vital matter, to a parting of the ways. The Eastern Church withdrew itself more and more from the affairs of men; the Western Church plunged deeper into them. Each took the consequences of its choice; Orthodoxy has remained divorced from history and culture, while Roman Catholicism and Protestanism have been constantly involved in the political and economic life of the West. You can maintain your integrity and purity, says Harnack, only at the price of ultimate sterility. You preserve your vitality at the cost of what must always seem to be moral compromise. Given these two options, most of us would agree that the latter is the less fatal to religion. You may, it is true, "cross your ancient blood with shame," but the life principle does not become extinct. I suggest, therefore, that when we deplore the secularized and vulgarised state of American Protestantism, we ponder for a while the consequences of an alternative choice, the sterility of a religion which is wholly otherworldly.*

I come now to what is, I think, the most difficult aspect of our whole subject—the everrenewed endeavour of a truly prophetic preacher

---

* Sensitive souls have always been aware of this dilemma. In his *Legenda Major* St. Bonaventure quotes words attributed to Saint Francis of Assissi: "What do ye counsel, Brethren, what do ye command? Shall I devote myself unto prayer, or shall I go about preaching? . . . Now in prayer, there seemeth to be the gain and heaping up of grace, in preaching, a certain giving out of the gifts received from Heaven; in prayer, again, a cleansing of the inward feelings, and an union with the one, true, and highest good, together with a strengthening of virtue; in preaching, the spiritual feet wax dusty, and many things distract a man, and discipline is relaxed. Finally, in prayer, we speak with God and hear Him, and live the life of angels, while we converse with angels; in preaching, we must needs practise condescension toward men and, living among them as fellow-men, must think, see, say, and hear such things as pertain unto men." Quot: *St. Francis of Assisi: 1226-1926: Essays in Commemoration.* London: University of London Press, Ltd., 1926, pp. 129-130.

to restore to his people the purity of the Christian ideal by courting for himself, and finally achieving, <u>professional martyrdom</u>. This martyrdom will normally take place, not as the result of theological heresy, but as a consequence of repeated attacks upon the political and economic conservatism of his people. No earnest minister can shut his eyes to the prospect of some such possible tragic ending to his career. There may be a point beyond which he cannot go, in his conformity to the common morals, and at which he must speak out.

Given the precedent of the major prophets and the pattern of prophecy at its best, the minister will often ask himself whether such martyrdom may not be his mission as well as his destiny. Unless the law of averages is to fail, "there be some standing here" who will eventually leave the Christian ministry of their own accord, or be forced out of it, because the complacency of the church seems to them incompatible with their Christian idealism. The thing has been happening for fifty years now and is likely to go on happening at an increasing pace. We might as well face the fact that no one of us has any guaranteed immunity to such a possible crisis in his own career. Let us, then, contemplate for a few moments all that is involved in this painful situation.

The man who enters the ministry ought to realize that the church is an institution. Most of the moral pioneering of history is done by free men, who are far in advance of the settled usages of their time. Their achievements, however, are ultimately preserved and consolidated in institutional form. Once the new idea of the pioneer has crystallized as an institution, the resulting fixed society is bound to be conservative. Having made good its initial case, Soviet Russia is today just as conservative as any other State; it must resist all change. No matter what organized society you live and work in, all are in this respect the same. Such is their nature, and their nature defines for them their duty. If any recognized member of an institution gets so far in advance of the rank and file of its membership that he becomes a liability rather than a help, the institution is bound either to recall him or to repudiate him.

To these general propositions the church is no exception. The Christian Church is jealous for its past; perhaps it lives too much in the past and too little in the future, but had it not been for the tremendous tenacity of the church to tradition it is a fair question whether Christianity would not have perished altogether. We do not see how it could have survived as the wholly unorganized life of unrelated individuals. In our holy impatience for a better world, we should remember that we cannot expect the church to move with the speed of a single man, not because specifically it is a church but because generically it is an institution.

Granted, however, that a prophetic preacher gets so far ahead of his people, or so far to one side of them, that the relation becomes difficult, what is he to do? Should he attempt to reestablish some working truce, or should he voluntarily cut the vital ties between himself and his people? Let me state the problem in its most classical instance. Was Jesus a suicide? Did he not only foresee the possibility of his death, but did he also deliberately plan and compel that death? Many of the more modern interpretations of the Synoptic Gospels suggest such a reading of the record. Most of us instinctively doubt that reading; we know that Jesus did not keep silence in order to avoid dying; we admit that he went up to Jerusalem with clear anticipation of the probable consequences of that journey; but we read out of the story more than was written into it, if we infer that either by word or deed he deliberately brought his cross upon his own shoulders.

The blood of the martyrs is said to have been the seed of the subsequent Christian Church. From the days of the first persecutions the church gloried in its martyrs, and, after they were dead, canonized them. But even in the days of fiercest tribulation the church never conceived of itself as a society of persons bound together by a compact to commit suicide. One of its problems was to prevent zealots from forcing the issue and exploiting in their own behalf its promise of heaven. Religion from time immemorial has been familiar with perverted natures who have insisted upon giving themselves unnecessary pain and doing themselves unwarranted harm. This trait in human nature is more characteristic of non-Christian asceticism than of sanctified Christian common sense. The church has never taught that the bare fact of physical martyrdom is a sure pass-key to heaven; it has always been the Christian's duty to stay unmartyred as long as he conscientiously could. The instinct which from the first prompted this working answer to a most difficult question is right. It is part, and a necessary part, of that feeling for the sacredness of all life which we believe to be inherent in the Gospel. Suicide and murder stand here upon the same ground.

The translation of this principle from the capital letters of actual martyrdom to the small letters of professional martyrdom in the ministry is not difficult. A man has no right to take his own ministerial life merely for the sake of so doing, for there is no assurance that such an act will be either the saving of his own soul or the conversion of the people.

At this point we must not abuse the patterns of true prophecy and genuine martyrdom. We gain nothing for ourselves or the cause by deliberately forcing the issue. There is a recognizable type of minister who goes about his world with a mounting grievance against the church. He is apt to feel himself lonely, misunderstood, and subject to petty persecution. Unless he is a man of wisdom and charity, he will let his troubles prey upon his mind. Turned in upon himself, he becomes more and more embittered and alienated from his people; he comes back to his pulpit Sunday after Sunday only to widen the gulf, and finally concludes that he had best hasten the unhappy logic of events to the only conclusion he can foresee.

It is an easy thing to kill yourself; a single bullet, one jump off a high bridge, a grain of poison will suffice. It is an equally easy thing to end, dramatically and abruptly, your career within an organized society. We shall always have the profoundest sympathy and respect for men who are genuine martyrs; but at this latest day we must, with the church of the earliest day, distinguish between two types—the one which is intent upon taking its own life, the other which in the end has its life taken from it. The instinct of the primitive church, when it first made the distinction, was psychologically sound, and we now have what the men of those days lacked, an apparatus for understanding that instinct. There is no moral obligation laid upon us to fall victims to a pathological martyr complex. The tendency, in the difficult conditions which we have been describing, to pity oneself, to dramatize oneself in public, and to do oneself mortal hurt, is in one form or another latent in us all. It is not a healthy trait in our natures, and its consequences are not necessarily a crown of righteousness to be awarded our characters.

I think, for example, of one man of a rather strongly ascetic bent, who wrote what he regarded as an ultra-radical book which he expected would bring on his professional martyrdom in the ministry. It failed to do so; his church knew him better than he knew himself and treated him gently. His book was declared to be interesting but not very important; he was at first puzzled and then vexed that he had failed to get himself put out of the church and the ministry. He was left in the awkward position of a man who has tried to commit suicide and who has waked up in a hospital where everyone is being kind to him—an annoying and humiliating experience.

We shall bring to our aid, therefore, in attempting to forecast our careers and to define our task in the ministry, the insights of the newer sciences of the human mind. We shall try to understand ourselves as well as our absolute idealisms. We shall, if we are sincere Christians, resist the insidious strains of self-pity and self-dramatization in our natures. We shall throw the burden of proof and action entirely upon the community.

A man has a duty as well as a right to sell his life dearly—even his professional life. If the hour should come when, in some hopeless controversy with the church, we realize that our ministry has come to an end, the act which ends it should be the act of the church and not our own act. We should stand clear, at that moment, of all suggestion of any lack of patience and charity, as of all suspicion of self-will and theatricality. The noblest martyrs have always been realists who at the last transcended the sentimentalism and romanticism of their immature life; I suspect also that the nearer they drew to the end the more nonresistant they became. In this tragic matter the burden of proof is on the church and not on us. Once we are ordained, it is our duty to remain in the ministry to the last possible moment. If we can take our professional life with a light hand, it is fair to say that we cannot have ever come alive to it, and have been wrongly placed from the first. A truly prophetic minister will never be a professional suicide, since the sacredness of his own professional life is the autobiographical form in which he tells the story of the sacredness of all life.

I wonder if you have been feeling, as you have been hearing these words, something of what I have felt in writing them—a certain lack of relevance to the situation in which we now find ourselves. We are the victims of the patterns in our own mind. Some of these patterns are theological, others are ethical. This pattern of the martyr-prophet is one with which Christian history is familiar and which is bequeathed to us with a certain moral obligation attending it. Yet it assumes on the part of the prophet an absolute certainty which is difficult to attain today, and on the part of the church a cruel lethargy which it is hardly fair to impute to it. Further-more, the suggestion that we can build up the church of the future, by exposing and disinte-grating the churches of the present, is at the moment a dubious strategy.

We are living at a time when those who are not "against" our religion must be counted "for" it. We are in Livingstone's dire extremity, "May God's richest blessing come down on any man" who "will help to heal" the ills of our time. Only a doctrinaire perversity will insist upon put-ting our churches out of bounds for such a pur-pose.

We are confronted today, the world over, not merely with the animal man who has always been our stubborn, persistent problem; we are con-fronted with reasoned apologias for the primitive instincts of the animal man. The dogma is a far more dangerous adversary than the brute human creature, because it has made the brute self-righteous as well as self-conscious. We all realize that the worst enemy which religion has to face in our own time is a rationalized system of belief and conduct dedicated to unspiritual and immoral ends. Europe is already torn to pieces by this issue, and we in America have no assurance that it may not be at any moment restated in the terms of our own life.

There is abroad today, as there has not been for the last four hundred years, a desire to close up the Christian ranks. The task of church union is not at the moment one which is to be prosecuted in the interests of financial economies or administrative efficiency. We need church unity for the sake of a common Christian mind. In our field nothing is more necessary than this. We ought to have a single Christian faith to profess, and substantial agreement on Christian ethics to oppose to the clean-cut dogmas of anti-Christ with which we are faced. A guerilla warfare conducted by brave and solitary individuals will not save the cause of Christianity, in the face of its consolidated modern enemies. The need is the greater because the more aggressive forces of the time have themselves the quality of a debased religion. You cannot dispose of a bad religion by attacking it as such; you can overcome it only by confronting it with a good religion. It must be answered in kind. But at the moment the members of the widely scattered Christian

Churches are hopelessly out of touch with one another and at variance regarding the meaning of their creed when it seeks ethical expression in the terms of race, sex, money, industry and the state.

There is a passage in one of the old Hebrew prophecies which says that "They that feared the Lord spake often one to another." In *Pirké Aboth 33* (Charles, A. and P. ii, 698) we read that R. Hanina b. Teradim said, "When two sit and there are not between them words of Torah, lo, this is 'the seat of the scornful,' as it is said: 'Nor sitteth in the seat of the scornful.' But when two sit and there are between them words of Torah, the Shechinah rests between them, as it is said: 'Then they that feared the Lord spake one with another.' " This is not a time in which religious men should be sitting in seats of scornful self-sufficiency. We need between us "words of Torah." We do not know each other's minds upon matters of faith and conduct nearly as well as we should; we ministers work in isolation; we preach our solitary sermons which we have conceived in our shut-in studies; we deliver them to the people or aim them at the people, who may take them or leave them as they choose. We do not consciously try to elicit the Christian mind of the congregation itself. We are merely confronting what we suggest to be its less Christian mind with what we assume to be our more Christian mind, and are leaving the matter there.

"The work of the ministry," says St. Paul, "is the edifying of the body of Christ." More particularly, and with direct reference to our immediate subject, "he that prophesies edifieth the church." Christian prophecy at its best differs here from Hebrew prophecy. The Hebrew prophet was traditionally a man who was tearing down a decaying and corrupt religious institution; the Christian prophet of the New Testament was a man who was building up a rising and still imperfect institution. St. Paul's picture of the prophet as a man who edifies the church is not one which naturally occurs to us; it is, however, the one which is most likely to suggest our best prophetic contribution to the present difficulties.

I find that many of my own contemporaries have lost most of their one-time interest in the prospect that they might become great preachers. "Great preaching," in the traditional sense of the word, was a transaction which belonged to the large leisure of more settled days than these. Great preaching will not save the cause of Christianity today. One of my friends said recently that the older you get the less you care about great men and the more you care about good men. Some such change is taking place in our interpretation of the modern sermon. Good preaching is more important today than great preaching. Good preaching will not call attention to itself or to the man who does it; it will, however, stir up the minds of the people and over a period of years will consolidate that mind into something like a common conviction and purpose. Good preaching will be self-effacing, sympathetic, and communal. It will, moreover, be conducted with a full awareness of what men in other churches are thinking and saying; it will be an attempt to substitute a single clear Christian voice for the babel of sounds which now issue from our divided and dissonant pulpits. The "edification of the church," in St. Paul's meaning of that phrase, is not a matter of better organization; it is not a matter of gratifying the palates of sermon tasters; it is a matter of eliciting one Christian mind and forming one Christian purpose as the church's answer to the aggression of the debased religions of these troubled times.

CHAPTER V

The Cult of Unconventionality

THE ideal sermon of today is less formal, more simple and direct, than that of a generation ago.

Indeed, a growing scepticism as to the use and worth of all sermons throws the emphasis, in certain types of church, toward the sacraments. Most of us who belong to the non-sacramental churches are increasingly aware that we are neglecting to our own loss this traditional means of grace. A strong feeling for sacraments is characteristic of persons and societies mature enough to have outgrown the hope of ever putting their faith into verbal formulas. All such prefer to have spiritual realities intimated by symbols rather than mutilated by words. A kindred preference for symbolism is found among those whose interests are predominantly aesthetic, or whose daily life is so much a matter of signs that the sacrament is religiously more congenial than anything spoken from a pulpit.

Each of us instinctively assumes that religion comes to everyone else as it comes to him, and means to others what it means to him. The wider our circle of friendship among religious men, the more impossible it is to maintain the assumption. To find your axioms challenged or denied is at first a perplexing experience, but ultimately a salutary discipline. Here is a reason for having close friends outside your own communion. Personally, I have learned more about Christianity from such friends than from my fellow denominationalists.

To discover, and then to admit, that there are people who do not go to church to hear a sermon means for some of us a change little less than revolutionary in our thinking. The truth is, however, that there are many Christians who get little or nothing from sermons and very much from the Eucharist. We, who celebrate or partake of the Lord's Supper only infrequently, find it hard to understand the man who must "make his communion" daily, if his Christian life is to be sustained. It is well for those of us who, as ministers, are more often in the pulpit than at the altar to admit that professionally we are in a minority. The bulk of the Christian Church rests upon the sacramental system.

On the other hand, there still are in our immediate world many persons who will be more helped by sermons than by sacraments. Given the dullness of so many of our sermons we may wonder that the preference persists and that the church has survived so long the heavy handicap of bad preaching. We might conclude that an *opus operatum* theory of preaching matches a like account of sacraments. In any case we, who have to preach and on the whole believe in preaching, need not fear lest we be left without hearers—if we have anything to say. The average American Protestant who goes to church, whether he is justified in his desire or not, wishes to hear a sermon and feels cheated if he is short-changed from the pulpit.

We are further reassured when we remember that the primitive Christian mission depended on preaching as its chief means of propaganda. It was the prophet rather than the priest who first spread the gospel. Human nature cannot have altered so radically that the original vehicle is now out-moded. Therefore we go back to the New Testament for suggestions as to the nature of our sermons and for reassurance as to their worth.

St. Paul is unequivocal:

For whosoever shall call on the name of the Lord shall be saved.

How then shall they call on him in whom they have not believed? and how shall they believe in him of whom they have not heard? and how shall they hear without a preacher?

The answer to the questions is obvious—there must be sermons. But the answer is in advance of the facts. The modern minister may not leap to the comfortable conclusion that his way of speaking in church on Sunday is a replica of Apostolic practice, certain to have the Apostolic effect. The difference is this—the word "sermon" and the whole idea which requires it are wanting in the New Testament.

A sermon is a formal discourse. The nearest approach in the New Testament to words so conceived is the speeches of the book of Acts, and as they stand those speeches are the work of a literary editor, not a verbatim record of what was said on the occasion. The first and second Christian generations were wholly innocent of the art of homiletics. Perhaps they were fortunate to have antedated all such sophistication. Studied preparation for preaching, and studied delivery of the sermon, came into the church at a later time as part of its heritage from the Graeco-Roman world. The literary ancestry of the conventional sermon should be sought in the classical schools of rhetoric, not on the mount of the Beatitudes. The Christian preaching of the early church must have been as artless as is witness in a Friends' Meeting today.

Preaching in that day differs from preaching now in another and far more important way. The two words habitually used in the New Testament to describe the transaction indicate the difference. The primitive preacher was either an "evangelist" who told good news, or a "herald" who made a proclamation. In either case he was one who announced to the world something which it had not known before, and which supposedly it was glad to hear. There was actual novelty in the words of the Christian herald and evangelist. It is true that belief in God, something like a sense of sin and a hunger for salvation, were common to Jew and Gentile. The actual novelty of the Apostolic preaching lay, not in its religious theories, but in its statement of a fact; the hope had been realized, the Messiah had come, the Word had been made flesh. "He suffered under Pontius Pilate, was crucified, dead, and buried. The third

day he rose again from the dead, he ascended into heaven."

The first Christian preachers trusted this amazing proclamation to get its own results. The early church had no ecclesiastical machinery of our kind to consolidate and to conserve the impression made by its missionary pronouncements. The passage from the Epistle to the Romans just quoted suggests that, in spite of many rebuffs, St. Paul persisted in the conviction that once men had heard the news, they would accept it and live by it. This was the strength of the first Christian preaching, its possession of a fresh truth of fact which was incontrovertible and important. Theoretically the hearer should welcome the gospel, since he ignored it to his peril and to his loss.

At this late date we are prohibited from doing what the first Christian preachers did. No man is denied an opportunity to give originality to Christian truth; he is, however, save under rarest conditions in remotest mission fields, denied the chance of announcing it as a novelty. We believe that there is between the first century and the twentieth century an unbroken continuity of organic Christian life. This living continuity, rather than formal recurrence or exact reproduction of any period of the Christian past, the first century in particular, is our chief present right to the term "Christian." Historically minded pietists are much too apt to suppose that they can imitate and thus reproduce definitive golden periods from the Christian yesterdays—the Reformation era, Franciscan times, the Apostolic age, the earthly days of the Son of Man. That is a false supposition and a mistaken approach to any event in past history. George Macaulay Trevelyan, writing of the period of the Commonwealth in England, says:

The feelings, speculations and actions of the soldiers of Cromwell's army are interesting in themselves, not merely as part of a process of "cause and effect" . . . For, irrespective of "cause and effect," we want to know the thoughts and deeds of Cromwell's soldiers, as one of the higher products and achievements of the human race, a thing never to be repeated, that once took shape and was. And so, too, with Charles and his Cavaliers, we want to know what they were like and what they did, for neither will they ever come again.[1]

The same may be said of the first Christian generation. It took shape and was, and will never be repeated. Therefore its sermons cannot be re-preached.

We might supplement Trevelyan's words, for

[1] *Clio, A Muse*, George Macaulay Trevelyan: Longmans, Green and Co., London, 1914, p. 13.

our own purposes, by a penetrating remark of Jung's:

> We Protestants must sooner or later face this question: Are we to understand the "imitation of Christ" in the sense that we should copy his life and, if I may use the expression, ape his stigmata; or in the deeper sense that we are to live our own proper lives as truly as he lived his in all its implications? It is no easy matter to live a life that is modelled on Christ's, but it is unspeakably harder to live one's own life as truly as Christ lived his.[2]

Liberal Protestant thought has not, in the main, come into the full liberty of the Christian man, as Jung so courageously conceives it. There is still the lingering desire to copy a model rather than to release a spirit. We are lodging in a half-way house between an imitative bondage and an emancipated originality.

It is with Christian preaching, therefore, as it is with so much of the world's pioneering. There are splendid achievements which can be done once for the first time and can never be done a second time in precisely the same way. You cannot discover America twice, or be twice over the first man to stand at the North or the South Pole. There can be but one Columbus, one Peary, one

[2] *Modern Man in Search of a Soul*, C. G. Jung: Harcourt, Brace and Company, New York, 1933, p. 273.

Amundsen. So with our profession; there can be but one St. Paul, one first Apostolic generation proclaiming its tremendous novelty to a waiting world.

So far as his major message is concerned, the modern preacher is denied novelty. If his sermons are a succession of novelties they are sure to be trivial and ephemeral. The preacher's true task might be defined as a response to the trite demand of the gospel hymn, "Tell me the old, old story." Most of the technical difficulties of preaching have their origin in the necessity of repeating things you have already said many times before to persons who have heard them still more times, who, indeed, already know them, or ought to know them, in advance of all sermons. From this necessity the art of preaching sprang, with all its conventions and patterns. The sermon forms and rules which have been elaborated century after century are an attempt to help men solve the problem of saying decently and in order what must be said over and over again.

There is abroad today a deep persuasion that the sermon has all but died of artificiality. Certainly the average twenty- or thirty-minute discourse, produced in obedience to forms prescribed in a homiletics class, bears little relation to the informal and direct utterance of a prophet. The inference is plain: the sermon is being strangled by conventions and, if it is ever to breathe freely again, these conventions must be torn off. Here the elusive and imperious ideal of the prophet beckons us. The technical way to begin to be prophetic is to have the wit to abandon the formal patterns for preaching which are a straight jacket for the free spirit of religion. The prophet recalls us to his primal spontaneity and encourages us to our own unfettered informality.

Now, the obvious way to destroy the conventions is to ignore them altogether. That is what is happening in many a modern pulpit. In keeping with what have been the antinomian tempers of the last twenty years, there is growing up among us a deliberate cult of unconventionality in preaching. Many of the old rules for making sermons seem much too prim for our free and easy age. The released pendulum swings to the opposite extreme, and prompts men to abandon all attempt at literary or oratorical form. The one rule for making the most modern sermon is to have no rule. Of the more recent trends in preaching this cult of unconventionality is at the moment the most vital, the most interesting, and the most problematical.

How often have we found ourselves, draped in a decorous Geneva gown and self-imprisoned in the steel armour of the sermon style, envying the candor and audacity of David, "I cannot go with these; for I have not proved them, and David put them off." Would that we had the courage to slough off the traditional mannerisms of the pulpit and to do the natural thing in the natural way. Those five smooth stones which David took from the brook, familiar to the hand and proved in the sling, ought to be sufficient charter for informality even to this day.

We know well enough what we are trying to do. We are trying to save the sermon from dying by inches of a kind of literary arthritis. As Coleridge once put it,

> Truths, of all others the most awful and interesting, are too often considered as so true, that they lose the power of truth, and lie bed-ridden in the dormitory of the soul, side by side with the most despised and neglected errors. [Our task is] to restore a commonplace truth to its first uncommon lustre.

Dr. Jacks has called this task the recovery of "The Lost Radiance of the Christian Religion." This recovery or restoration, so far as we can see, will be best effected by means of more spontaneous preaching. The beginning of our quest shall be a denial of the homiletic idols to which we have so long bowed down. Our new cult of unconventionality announces itself, therefore, by deliberate practices which suggest its rebel intention. There shall be no Bible passage as a point of departure; there certainly shall be no text, since that is one of the most deadening devices handed down from the past; there shall be no attempt at anything like introductions and conclusions; there shall be a wholly colloquial vocabulary and a most conversational manner.

One of the pioneers of this cult is a well-known religious leader who confided to me some five years ago: "I have wholly given up trying to preach a sermon in the usual sense of the word. I go into the pulpit without any special preparation and talk to people informally about whatever happens to be uppermost in my mind." Such a procedure is not a further pruning of the branches of the homiletic tree in an attempt to make it still more symmetrical; it is an axe laid at the root of the whole process. Should we be better preachers if we had the courage to follow his example?

The man whom I have just cited differs from most of us in that he is not now, and never has been, a parish minister. He is a free lance, who

seldom speaks twice to the same congregation.
Given his constantly changing audiences his method
is effective. His addresses—they can hardly be
called sermons—have an intimate quality which
instantly catches the attention. His halting process
of thinking out loud in your presence gives you
a fellow feeling for him. You labor with him as
his ideas come to reluctant birth in sentences. You
hunt with him for the word he cannot find. He
is an utterly sincere man and in all this stands
clear of any suggestion of conscious artifice. The
transaction is honest throughout, yet he has the
advantage of availing himself unconsciously of
certain well-known ways of gaining attention
and keeping sympathy, which are rhetorical devices hoary with age.

His hearers in the meantime are exhilarated
by their experience. A great man has done them
the honor of inviting them to share with him the
formulation of his thought. They realize that
they may even be participating with him in the
conception of his next book. They know that
first-hand thinking is going on in their presence.
The preacher is not reading to them sentences
he put down on paper the previous Thursday,
or repeating by rote words he memorized on Saturday. He is not even consulting his notes. The

very genesis of ideas is taking place here and now.

The preacher in question, because he has no parish, appears in a pulpit only as an invited guest. The resident minister must always be of two minds about asking him; on the one hand, in the interests of his church attendance he cannot afford not to ask him if he can get him; on the other hand, he knows only too well how he is going to suffer by contrast. The local man sits humbly in his place in the chancel, listening with his fellow members to this new note of preaching, and becomes in their eyes a flagrant and a public example of how not to preach. The congregation leaves the church with mingled sighs of satisfaction at what it has just heard and of impatience with what it regularly has to hear. Should we then burn our text books and our lecture notes on preaching, as belonging to some black magic, and go into the pulpit as this man goes, free and unfettered, rejoicing in a mature informality?

The implications and ramifications of the question are many. They reach out far beyond sermon methods, and concern our whole interpretation of the art of life. If it be the office of religion to unify character, we ought, as religious men, to be consistent; our way of meeting the world and of handling experience should run true to form whatever be the concern of the moment. When we inaugurate a cult of unconventionality in preaching, are we prepared to extend that cult to the conduct of the rest of life, and to stand by the consequences?

Affirmation of a right to be unconventional may be an instinctive struggle for freedom. Perhaps we have been cabined, cribbed, confined by the dead hand of the past or by the pressure of social custom around us. We feel that if ever we are to find ourselves, we must break loose. Some such motive undoubtedly lies behind the rebel tempers and acts of each oncoming youthful generation.

Century after century men have felt a need of conscientious irreverence toward existing religious forms, for the sake of achieving personal religion. We have all known these moods. The profounder expressions of this holy impatience we identify as nonconformity. The whole subject of the nonjuring, non-coöperating, and nonconforming person is one that needs careful study in the light of what we now know about the tricks which the unconscious plays upon our conscious thoughts and choices. I know of no adequate treatment of the subject, and were one to be had it would throw much light on places which are now dark. I offer the theme without private copyright as the substance of a doctoral thesis to any properly qualified graduate student in theology.

Plainly we are dealing here with a constant type, which is recognizable and which may be trusted to react to life in accordance with its own rules. Unconventionality becomes, sooner rather than later, an easily identified convention, and the manners of its advocates are quite as predictable as the easy-going habits of the wicked world against which it holds itself to be a vital protest. The reaction of the convinced pacifist or communist to the existing world order is as automatic and as uniform as that of the purse-proud bondholder or the benighted militarist. There is nothing to be gained from cherishing the illusion that the latter are conventional persons and the former unconventional—as types they both run true, each to its own form.

Why do men get at cross purposes with their world? What is the secret of their conventional unconventionality? Plainly their attitude is not always necessitated by major abuses in their environment. Many men are chronic non-coöperators, who may be trusted to dissent from any proposition which is made to them, however innocent or feasible. Why was it, for example, that Emerson loved the "Nay-sayer" better than the "Yea-sayer"? We can understand how persons who are unclassed should be against the existing order. But why Emerson? He was lord of all he surveyed in Concord, an honored Wise Man throughout the land. In his person he had no grudge against society. What native need or social occasion had he for his dissidence of dissent? It would seem that the answer to this problem is not to be sought in social or political facts, but in the recesses of what St. Augustine calls our "remembered forgetfulness," accessible only to the psychologist. We shall be much in debt to anyone who will explore for us this obscure area of human character. We cannot affirm that "Naysaying" is in the order of nature, for within a single species mutual aid is the law of animal life, and our uncorrupted instinct would incline us to coöperate with our kind rather than to withhold our coöperation. Whence, then, and why, the nonjuror, the non-coöperator, the nonconformist, save in the presence of abuses so obvious that any decent man must recoil from them?

May it be that the very word "Protestant" and

the hereditary genius of our common Protestantism have bred in us a fixed habit of taking exception to the catholic, *i.e.*, the universal—facts with which we are confronted? I raise these questions because they have more than an academic interest. We have just concluded two great œcumenical Conferences, one on Life and Work, the other on Faith and Order, held in Oxford and Edinburgh last summer. I violate no secret in saying that there is abroad among the liberal Protestant Churches of America a scepticism as to the worth of such gatherings. This scepticism is said to rest upon an inability on our part to allow the more conservative churches of Europe to impose upon us the theological tests which they still require—a Nicene Creed or an Augsburg Confession. Does it occur to us that the difficulties which such conferences face may have their origin quite as much in our temperamental inclination to hold aloof and stay apart as in the theological formulas of the more orthodox? If such symbols are, as in their letter they are for many of us, a hindrance rather than a help to reunion, so also are our own hereditary tempers with which we approach these gatherings. Why are we like that? I wish I knew. I am sure that the attitude is not a splendidly consistent virtue. If the protestant type has had its great occasions and its signal triumphs, it has had also its sham battles and its hollow victories. Hence the need that at this point psychology should come to the aid of history.

This digression to ponder the riddle of the "Nay-sayer" will not be irrelevant if it serves to put us on our guard, as preachers, against the conclusion that a studied neglect of homiletic tradition will ensure us membership in the historic society of true prophets. It will take more than cavalier manners in the pulpit to induct us into that austere company. The cult of unconventionality in preaching falls short of anything like passionate nonconformity, and had best be considered at its own level and in its own terms. Primarily it is, and indeed is usually employed as, a matter of professional strategy. The problem is a technical one, that of finding the best means of saying effectively what we wish to say. I propose, therefore, to deal with the cult of homiletic unconventionality in such terms.

Let us admit that the itinerant preacher may be well advised to cultivate the informality of which we have been speaking. He stands before an audience once or twice. He depends in part upon his skill and wit to gain a hearing for his words. The settled minister in a parish depends, and should depend, upon the confidence which people have in him as a man. Such confidence inclines them to listen with sympathetic interest to anything he has to say. They welcome his ideas because they trust him. In the case of the occasional speaker no such confidence can exist, or, if it exists, it rests upon report and not upon repeated personal verification. Therefore the roving preacher is forced to make the case for his sermon by means of the impression of the moment. He must gain attention at once and he must sustain interest through the few minutes that he speaks. He cannot afford to hamper himself with rhetorical rules of any kind. He must break through them and reach at once the minds and hearts of the listeners.

He is, therefore, warranted in deliberately cultivating unconventionality. All of us who have occasion, from time to time, to do speaking of this sort are quite aware that we allow ourselves under such circumstances liberties of style which we deny ourselves when we are about our year-in-year-out work in our own fields. This is not hypocrisy, it is not insincerity, it is not even "preaching-down" to persons whom we do not know. It is a candid recognition of the uniqueness

of a situation in which comparative strangers
face each other for a single hour and must establish as intimate and complete an understanding as that brief time allows. We might liken
such a meeting to the friendships we occasionally
make on a sea voyage. Under such circumstances
we sometimes have courage to be more natural
and outspoken than is our daily wont. The situation invites candor. But you always realize that
you are speaking so freely and telling so much,
precisely because the friendship is to be a matter
of a few days rather than of many years. You
would not and you could not wear your heart
on your sleeve so openly all the time; it would
get weather-beaten and certainly would be abused
if it was so constantly exposed. God has provided
our best bodily armour for our brains and our
heart. The rest of our bones are inside; our skulls
and our ribs are outside, presumably for some
good purpose—perhaps to suggest the need of
proper protection for our deepest ideas and our
strongest feelings.

The real issue to be faced by those who deliberately affect the cult of homiletic unconventionality is this: "How will the method wear?" It
is effective when a man is a newcomer in a parish. But will it be as effective at the end of a

ten-year ministry as at its beginning? Many of its present-day exponents are prepared to cast their lot with the method for an indefinite period. In the modern pulpit we have not yet had long enough trial of this cult of unconventionality to say what its "survival value" is. We shall know twenty-five years hence whether the modern informal sermon is the success which at the moment it seems to be.

For myself, I can only enter certain reservations and suspicions. The method can and will succeed for an indefinite time with the indubitable saint or genius. One cannot imagine being uninterested in anything that Henry Thoreau might have said. His unconventionality was fresh every morning. The method can be trusted to succeed for an appreciable time with a preacher who is a skilful craftsman. It carries within it, however, an ineradicable germ of insincerity. Behind the innocent suggestion of uncalculated speech there lies conscious artifice. Once you realize that this is so, your confidence in a preacher is subtly destroyed.

My mother once described to me hearing in New York the same sermon preached in three different churches by one of the reputedly great preachers of the last century. His name is known to you all, but since the rule *de mortuis nil nisi bonum* is binding, I withhold the name. At a given point in the sermon, as first heard, he hesitated for a word, and said, "What is the word I want?" The congregation leaned forward with eager sympathy to shout the word he could not find, and settled back with a sigh of relief when he got it for himself. He did precisely the same thing at the same moment in the same sermon on a second occasion, and again on a third, with like effect in each of the latter cases. With like effect save upon one woman, who realized that the transaction was not honest, and who therefore lost moral confidence in a man for whom she had previously had the greatest respect. Once a congregation suspects and then slowly realizes that the unconventionality of your preaching is studied and not spontaneous, you have done yourself mortal hurt as their helper. Preaching can survive countless honest errors; it cannot stand insincerity.

The devotees of the cult of unconventionality must therefore reckon with the fact that they cannot permanently silence the suspicion that the transaction is not what it seems to be, and that art is being employed in what seems at first to be the artless expression of a direct and candid nature. Personally I have no objection to the obvious employment of literary art in a sermon; indeed, I do not think that a lifetime's preaching can be done in neglect of art. I do object, however, to a man's giving me to understand that he has scrapped all the arts in an attempt to return to nature and then employing in the exposition of his naturalness one of the most sophisticated of all the forms of art, a studied informality.

The question comes down in the end to this: Can the constantly recurring ideas, feelings, acts of a human life, in church as well as out of church, be negotiated without final resort to conventions of some kind? I doubt it. These constant, elemental and repeated concerns must be recognized and dealt with by words, gestures, ceremonies. We meet each other when the day begins, and part from each other when day ends. The two moments call for verbal recognition. Custom suggests that we say "Good morning" and "Good night." The unconventionalist is irked by these formal phrases; they seem to him lifeless and heartless. He therefore turns his back upon them and adopts vivid alternatives. He greets you when day begins with a "Cheerio" and parts from you when it ends with a "Well, so long." His manner is informal and intimate. Yet after a while the matutinal "Cheerio" gets on your nerves. It is as punctual as the sun and as liturgical as any older formula. You are not certain whether he is proving his case, making you feel his vivid personality as he so evidently wishes to do. In effect he has given up an old convention, has achieved for a while an attractively informal vocabulary, only to turn his unconventional formula into a new convention. The question then arises, and it is a difficult question for him and all concerned, whether for the purposes of human nature's daily need the new convention is a better one than the old. It may be, but there is no guarantee.

Let us take a more explicit example from our own field. The ordinary church service is fairly formal, and its formality often seems to be its gravest liability. What is the answer? To break away and start an unconventional service, let us say an evening service. From this impulse came the Sunday Evening Forum movement, which has spread across the country. Its parent, perhaps, is Ford Hall in Boston. But Mr. Coleman, who has been the wise guide of Ford Hall over many years, told me the other day that so far as informality and spontaneity at Ford Hall are concerned, they are now in danger of becoming ancient history. The evening proceedings have crystallized into a recognized pattern, the naked palpitating thing it once was has secreted a shell around itself. Thus, he went on to say, at a stated moment in the program, the same radical has risen from the same seat in the balcony and asked the same question every Sunday night for a dozen years. The questioner is as ceremonial as a priest and his words are now as liturgical as any printed in a prayer book. Ford Hall is thus faced with the problem whether this ceremonial act and liturgical question serve the long cause of religion better than the deeds and words of a traditional church. It is no longer a matter of unconventionality against conventionality, but rather of the relative merits of two conventions employed to serve substantially the same interest.

The initial appeal of the Oxford Group meetings rests upon their informality and apparent spontaneity. Here are people being natural in the name of religion, rather than artificial. But one shrewd observer suspected the spontaneity was specious:

Most of the confessions had all the signs of a carefully prepared performance. Though the production was clever, the utter lack of reverence made it singularly ineffective. Jokes were made with the regularity of those in a vaudeville house.

My original suspicion proved justified when I went to other meetings and discovered the same young men and women, confessing the same sins, repeating the same jokes, forcing the same laughter and interruptions from a *claque* distributed cleverly in the hall.[3]

For the student of contemporary religion, much of the interest and significance of the Group Movement depend upon the pace with which the Groups are making their own ecclesiastical history. They are passing through, in a short time, a consecutive history which has taken traditional churches a much longer time. Their first evangelical period seems to be over; they are already in their "apostolic" age, in which usages are becoming fixed and tradition settled. They have now to face for the future of the movement the serious problem of the permanent, survival value of "young men and women, confessing the same sins, repeating the same jokes, forcing the same laughter." Ten years hence, to say nothing of fifty years hence, the jokes may have begun to wear thin, and the laughter become hollow. The new unconventionality may prove a poor permanent convention.

Let us hear the conclusion of the whole mat-

[3] *God Is My Adventure*, Rom Landau: Alfred A. Knopf, 1936. p. 183.

ter. <u>Unconventionality, as a studied strategy, has
no advance guarantee of indefinite life</u>. Any man
can be unconventional for a short while, and on
this basis can have a temporary success. We are
thinking, however, not of a circuit-riding ministry
but of a lifetime to be spent in a half dozen
parishes. We are thinking also, not of personal
reputation and following, but of those far more
important matters, the communication of the Christian religion and the steady increment of the
church.

The difficulty with the cult of unconventionality
is this; when we are properly employed about
the concerns which are committed to our charge
we are dealing with a few constantly recurring
experiences, ideas, emotions, purposes, and needs
which man has always associated with religion.
It would be irrelevant in the sermon to talk about
the weather. Book reviews are a poor substitute.
Our contributions to the political and economic
wisdom of society are not uniformly important.
<u>But we are supposed to know something about
the divine discontent which gnaws forever at the
heart of man, making him a pilgrim and stranger
on the earth</u>. And we have to put these deep, constant, recurring concerns into words, and deal with
them Sunday after Sunday. They are so ingrained

in man that they are never sloughed off or out-grown. Here is our province, and it is a province where technically the permutations and combinations of ideas, so far from being infinite are, indeed, rather limited. Unconventional ways of dealing with these ideas are bound to exhaust themselves soon. The most and the best that the average man does is to substitute his own less formal ways of doing and saying the traditional thing for the more formal one against which he is in revolt.

In the end he will arrive, merely from exhaustion of his resources, at some recognized, recurring way in which he will preach a sermon. He cannot avoid creating his own patterns. Unpatterned preaching over a lifetime, indeed over more than a very short period of time, is a technical impossibility. We had best make our peace with the fact that the period of unconventionality in any serious life, particularly in the life of an historic religion, is brief. In this matter of sermon forms we cast off our too narrow and rigid shells, are soft-shelled for a short time only, and then begin at once again to secrete new shells. This is a psychological necessity from which none of us has any escape.

We might as well, then, begin and continue

our preaching with the candid admission that sermons cannot be permanently unpatterned utterances. We are not under bonds to be slavishly subservient to old homiletic patterns, but we must recognize the inevitability of the principle of pattern. I end with a dogmatic statement which is worth what it is worth—most of man's beautiful and permanently enduring creations have been wrought within a pattern and in conscious consent to it, rather than in deliberate neglect of it.

CHAPTER VI

Our Professional Skills

WE REALIZE with regret that the ministry as a profession does not have the influence in the community which once it had. The world at large discounts both us and our utterances; for the most part we are good naturedly tolerated. On stated public occasions we are still traditionally necessary; in times of private extremity we are urgently summoned. Now and then, when we make an unconventional statement about public affairs, we are copy for the newspapers. Otherwise our week-in and week-out words no longer carry the weight which once they had.

The situation is a complex one. Common report has it that our breed has declined. The world forgets, however, how many men in the old days drifted into the ministry along a line of least resistance. That drift has stopped and is setting in other directions. The one sufficient motive for going into the ministry today is a personal concern for the ideas with which it deals, and a desire to bring those ideas to bear upon the life of men and women around us.

There is at present a dearth of great preachers. That situation has changed, and if great preachers are the measure of the ministry it has changed for the worse, even within our memory. But there is a dearth of great men everywhere. The truth is, not that the best men in the world are men of smaller stature than their predecessors, but that the level of general attainment has risen in the community as a whole. The contrast between the best men and those of average parts is not so sharp as once it was. Moreover, this is a difficult time in which to be a great man. It was a swift and accurate insight into the present nature of our world which, after the war, led the nations to honor their unknown soldiers rather than their well-known generals. Only anonymity can compass vast dimensions of contemporary events. Our professional hero today might very well be the obscure country minister rather than the famous city preacher.

Let me hazard a further guess as to the dilemma in which we find ourselves. The trouble is not with our basic selves, but with an interpretation of our calling into which we have been unwittingly forced. The broadened definitions of

liberal religion, which make it coextensive with
the whole of life, have increased our opportunities and duties so that all of man's affairs are
our proper concern. Therefore our interest and
efforts scatter widely. Our forbears in the ministry went hunting with a rifle. We go hunting
with a double-barrelled shot gun; if there were
such a thing I should say a multiple-barrelled
shot gun. We are handy men and jacks-of-all
trades in a world of skilled workers. We are concerned for the whole of life in an age which
has been preoccupied with departments of life.
We are dealing with imponderables in a day when
men are impatient of anything which cannot be
weighed and measured. I might put the distrust
of us in two remarks made to me recently. A
thoughtful woman said, "I do not go to church
because I cannot stand the reckless statements
made in hymns and prayers and sermons upon
the most abstruse matters. No one can possibly
know as much as you ministers suggest that you
know." A distinguished scholar declined an invi-
tation to conduct morning prayers in the college
chapel because, as he put it, "I never speak in
public upon matters on which I cannot feel that
I have something like exact knowledge, and such
knowledge is not possible in religion." Anything

that you and I can say to such persons—and
they are the persons who are doing the serious
work of the modern world—seems to them either
so presumptuous or so inexact that we do not
command their confidence. When they listen to
us preach they do not feel that intellectually
they are on solid ground. Our age is, in George
Meredith's phrase, "hot for certainties," and the
words of religion seem merely the "dusty an-
swers" of a confessed uncertainty. We are the
practitioners of an inexact art in a time which
has put its trust in exact sciences.

The fault is not wholly ours; it is in equal
part the fault of our critics. In so far as we are
citizens of our own time and have been touched
by its mental tempers, we can understand the
difficulties which men have with any religion and
all religion. Our age is trying to make knowledge
do duty for faith, and is half ashamed to say that
it believes where it cannot know. We shirk the
residual element of mystery in the universe. We
prefer the cheerful light which shines within the
four walls of restricted certitudes to the deep
darkness of the open night. A genteel conspiracy
of silence surrounds most of the topics with which
religion has been traditionally concerned. It is
hardly good form to tell a man that he has sinned.

Men no longer do wilful wrong; they are the victims of their heredity, of their unconscious selves, or of their environment. They are to be pitied, not blamed. Our age is sentimental and essentially dishonest about death. We cannot look with level eye at its face of cold clean ivory. Priding ourselves on our fearless realism, we are wholly unrealistic in the presence of the "last enemy." We muse in private upon the possibility that there may be some life after this, but our reflections seldom bear on the conduct of this present life, and we keep our personal hopes and fears to ourselves. To mention the possibility of one's own immortality is construed as a slightly improper self-interest, something which the socially minded altruist does not do. At the most "it comforts us to know that truth abides," even though the truth takes toll of our lives in the process of surviving. Altogether, being aware of these mental traits in ourselves, we can understand the widespread and studied indifference to the themes with which the ministry must deal. Amos was not the only prophet who has been advised to go somewhere else and preach to less sophisticated circles. There are today many subjects which it is not good manners to mention at the king's court and in the king's chapel of the accepted intellectual conventions.

Our situation, however, is not without its elements of hope. Whatever else we may stand for, we stand for the whole of life, both the life of the individual and the lives of all sorts and conditions of men in an ideal society. Ours has been a thankless job in an age of specialization, but the dreariest hours of our vigil may be over. Men are finding, in increasing numbers, that no single certitude within any one restricted area of knowledge, nor the sum of all such certitudes, can give them a final meaning for life or fullness of wisdom for living. The age of science, particularly in its most recent forms, has divided and sub-divided our experience until life has well nigh lost all value and even its very reason for being. There is a growing demand in many quarters that once again we be allowed to "see life steadily, and see it whole." A day of better things is in store for any man—be he poet, painter, musician, or preacher—who stands for the ideal of unity. Men are bringing back to him the dismembered fragments of their experience, and asking him to restore to them their lost feeling for life's wholeness and singleness.

We shall, however, misconstrue our contemporaries, and therefore fail them, if we assume that they are returning to us as penitent prodigals or empty-handed travelers. We have been stewards of the whole of life, commanded to watch over the deepest concerns of the human spirit while the modern mind has been journeying in far countries of specialized research. But the mind of our time has not been wasting its substance in riotous living in a far country. It has learned some things which are precious and which it will not renounce if rebuked by the church. There are in the *Apocrypha* two sayings which throw no little light on our present situation. One is found in *Ecclesiasticus*, "Wisdom raineth down skill." The other occurs in *The Wisdom of Solomon*, "The very true beginning of her [*i.e.*, wisdom] is the desire of discipline."

We are living in a time when it has "rained down skill." The skills of the modern world have not yet been correlated or brought within the jurisdiction of a moral, much less a spiritual, interpretation. Yet they have in them the promise of the ethics and the religion of tomorrow. They reveal a potentially religious quality which no sensitive man can miss, even though they are innocent of any theological vocabulary. You cannot go into modern factories, laboratories, libraries, hospitals without realizing, with an ever fresh wonder, how exact the processes of the modern mind have become and how skilful men are at the major trades and professions. A passion for precision, and in many instances an approximate attainment of the ideal, is widespread. This is, I think, one of the hopeful and redeeming features of a time which otherwise has countless glaring defects.

How do men achieve these skills? Another phrase from the Wisdom literature gives us our answer—by "a holy spirit of discipline." The true beginning of their skills has been in the sciences a desire of discipline, and in the trades a necessitated acceptance of discipline. The undisciplined and unskilled workman is an anachronism. In want of technical ability a man cannot hope to survive in the kind of world in which we are now living and apparently are to go on living.

Such is the situation with which we ministers are confronted. It creates a new problem for us and makes new demands upon us. A general culture, which was once the minister's best professional equipment, is hardly adequate for the present occasion. It condemns one so often to the society of persons who are intellectually second-rate. We should like to be preaching to the skilled brain workers at one extreme and the skilled hand workers at the other extreme, yet these two classes are the most conspicuous absentees from church. They do not stay away because they are uniformly uninterested in religion; many of them think and care about such matters deeply. They are, in part, kept away by the pressure of their own work which is exacting and wearing. They are, perhaps, too content to shut themselves up with their restricted tasks, and their self-confinement must prove in the end their error and their loss. But I suspect that they are discouraged about church-going mainly because, on their occasional visits to churches, they do not meet in the person of the preacher a mind of precision equal to their own. They do not expect to find an identical mind; they do wish to recognize a kindred mind.

Some time ago our friend J. Edgar Park, who was your last Lyman Beecher lecturer, came down here to Yale for the dedication of a new physics building. He said that, as he went through the laboratory and saw the delicate apparatus with which the routine work of modern physics is done, he realized by contrast how inexact the processes of our minds are in making and preaching sermons. We have all had just such sobering experiences.

For eight years I sat on Sunday mornings in the chancel of a church in Boston looking down the length of the main aisle at a head usher standing by the door. He was always tired and often unfit to be out. He was by profession a chartered accountant. His days, and long hours of his nights, were spent in the service of mathematical precision. Many a Sunday I suspected that he had been in his office until midnight on Saturday, hunting for the few elusive pennies to balance an account, or poring over the faked entries of some defaulting bookkeeper. As I looked at him I was rebuked by my willingness to appear in church with a sermon which I knew was only half prepared. I felt morally ill at ease and inferior. Yet such are the persons on whom, in increasing numbers, we look out in a modern congregation. They have their disciplines, their precisions, their skills, and their proper pride.

What have we to offer them? Well, we have no right to insult them with the standard sentence which has been our homiletic stock in trade—"How truly this principle is illustrated in the lives of Isaiah, St. Paul, St. Francis, Savonarola, and David Livingstone." Consider that sentence for a moment. No possible meaning can be got out of it because no thought went into it. It sounds like a series of door-bells ringing in an apartment house where everyone is out. The human mind can hardly identify those proper names, when spoken in a single sentence, much less give content to them. We smile superciliously at the Tibetans who pin their petitions to a prayer wheel and leave them to be blown round by the wind. But in our preaching we often pin idle sentences to a sermon wheel, hoping that they may work as magic incantations. I cannot see that a preacher has a moral right to offer people in the twentieth century any such hollow verbal formula. We cannot blame a clear-thinking lawyer, or a hard-working laborer, if he feels instinctively that he has outgrown the day when such pulpit rhetoric can do duty as religion.

Or, once again, there was in the old evangelical days a tacit agreement that no sermon was complete unless it made obeisance to the cross. Therefore, in most sermons there was a final paragraph about the atoning death of Christ, which was appended indiscriminately to all sermons on all subjects. Looking back, we can see that this was not passionate faith: it was a homiletic convention. Human nature, in the ministry as elsewhere, is curiously constant. There is abroad today a suggestion that no sermon has fulfilled its mission unless it makes passing or final mention of the economic and industrial situation on the one hand, and of the international situation on the other hand. Why rid ourselves of an old convention merely to fall victims to a new one? There may not be at present any other subjects so well worth discussing as these, but in that case they deserve more than a paragraph's mention; they deserve a whole sermon. Indeed, they deserve two sermons, one for each! Even at that he would be a very bold man who assumed that in two sermons he could touch the common conscience deeply or make any important contribution to the solution of these stubborn problems. We should have outgrown the idea that when we send our minds abroad from the pulpit they must never come home without having at least bowed to those two matters. Students in my own sermon delivery classes are now familiar with a rule which says that any man who solves both the social problem and the international problem in the final paragraph of the same sermon is failed in the course. We shall come back to these imperiously urgent and incredibly difficult issues again and again, but when we do so we shall try to deal with them honestly and seriously. We all know that, glorious as it was, the flight over Everest was not and never can be the same thing as an ascent of Everest. So, a rhetorical flight over the hard problems of economics and internationalism is not the same thing as a face to face attack upon them. We need in our preaching what one of the Everest climbers has called "close work on the face of the rock."

The instinct of self-defence is, however, strong in us, and we are ready to give an account of the cause of our want of precision in preaching. Sermons are not mere recitations of fact; they are affirmations of belief. We are, like the artist, dealing with matters in which taste is even more important than information. In particular, it is our duty to pass those judgments of value which it is equally the duty of science to withhold. We are to be men of faith, going out into the unknown, not knowing whither we go. Therefore you cannot require of a sermon the same precision which you may properly demand of a lawyer's brief, or the same skill which you expect of a surgeon at a major operation. We do not and cannot work in areas where the exactness of the sciences is possible; therefore we do well to avoid what has been called "the fallacy of misplaced concreteness."

There is a measure of truth in this *apologia*, but there is also an element of danger. Faith is an expression of the creative energy of the mind rather than of its powers of observation. Science takes photographs; the arts and religion paint portraits. Yet in religion, as in the arts, we must distinguish between fancy and imagination. Fancy is the inventive power of the mind working without reference to fact. Imagination is the same power addressed directly to fact and eliciting from it more than it yields to observation. The artists are always careful to make and to keep this distinction. An artist may endow a sunrise or a sunset with the light that never was on land or sea. But he may not make his sun rise in the west and set in the east. The case has been well put by a critic writing long ago in the *Edinburgh Review* (April, 1849). A poet, he says, may be forgiven false sentiment, false passion, false logic, but

false description is a scandal to the outward senses: and if a poet plants his willows on the mountainside, or insists upon the yeomanly oak bathing its unbound tresses in the flowing stream—still more should his apples be bold enough to come "before the swallow dares" and his lambs begin to bleat for a better shepherd when "rivers rage and rocks grow cold"— he may possibly, if not very much in the fashion, fall in with readers who will object to being deceived with their eyes open.

An increasing number of persons in the pews object to being deceived from the pulpit as to matters of fact. Indeed, the trouble is that they are not deceived. They merely write down the preacher as a man who is ignorant or careless, and in either case not to be trusted. We underrate the damage we do to our influence and our cause by repeated mistakes as to matters of fact, or by patent ignorance of fact. The common mind is much more critical at this point than it was a generation or so ago.

We shall see ourselves as others see us if we consult our own reaction to writers and speakers. Let a man make a misstatement in some field with which we are familiar and we instantly put a question mark against him as one whose mental processes are not reliable. His pleasant style, his winning personality, the plausibility of his rhetoric—none of these can undo the distrust he creates in our minds when he is found in error as to what is actually so.

Here, for example, lying before me on the desk where I am writing, is a book review by a well-known dean in one of our eastern universities, described in the journal carrying his article as a man who "has taught and written much on the literature of modern languages." He tells us that " 'The noblest Monument of English Prose' is, of course, the St. James version of the English Bible." It may be the merest pedantry to take exception to his confusion of saints and kings, nevertheless that common error costs him much of your confidence.

If he knew no better, so much the worse for his reputation as a man of letters. If he merely made a slip of the pen, the slip should have been caught in proof-reading. If he failed to read his own proofs we put him down as a careless writer. Altogether, given his inauspicious reference to "Saint James" as the sponsor of the 1611 version, you would rather hear what someone else has to say about the English Bible.

This matter of care and conscience in dealing with citations of fact is the more important because all good preaching is concrete. One of the two or three most useful patterns for the sermon is that which proceeds by analogy from the natural to the spiritual. This was the way in which Jesus preached in the parables, but no one has ever suggested that his analogies fall to the ground because his accounts of actual life are inaccurate. We use as our points of departure not merely stories of common life; we use history and biography and adventure and literature and the stuff of the natural sciences. The inferences to be drawn at the higher level will be wholly invalidated if our account of the lower level is wrong.

Until we take the trouble to compare the characteristic American sermon with sermons preached in the Old World we do not realize how empirical our mental processes habitually are. Odell Shepard identifies this Yankee trait in the sermon-tasting habits of his hero, Bronson Alcott.

Alcott had no hesitation in speaking his mind, at least to himself, about the preachers of Boston. For he was an expert. Good preaching differed in no essential respect, he believed, from good teaching. In motive and method and effect it was the same thing. In method particularly; for it too must begin with something near and concrete and known—not with the universe but with the kitchen and shop, and not with "bravery" but with a brave deed. Upon that specific thing or deed it must generalize, of course, carrying the symbols of this always emblematic world as far as possible into the abstract realms of ultimate reality, and then it must return again to the shadowy but actual realm of here and now. Good teaching always showed this movement—from the known to the unknown and back, enriched, into the known. Good preaching must show it too.[1]

Any minister preaching to the average American congregation will do well to ponder these words, for they suggest the most serviceable of the many forms of sermon outline with which he can work.

To this matter-of-fact manner of the Yankee mind—which has always referred its transcendentalism back to the most homely concerns—the inductive methods of modern thought have given

[1] *Pedlar's Progress*, Odell Shepard: Little, Brown and Company, 1937, p. 119.

a further lease of life. For most thoughtful men in our time faith is a venture into the unknown suggested and even warranted by the nature of the known. Religion uses the same method as science, but carries it further. Now the flight of faith in that upper air which is its proper element is, to use a modern simile, not unlike the flight of a plane, which is in its element only when it is up; but in order to get it up it must take off from solid ground. It must have a straight run along a smooth, hard surface. So, while many of our religious beliefs are not earth-bound, they are earth-initiated. Precisely because we so constantly preach by analogy, we owe to the faith we purpose to profess preliminary care that the facts from which it takes off are reliable. Otherwise our inferences and our analogies come to nothing in the common mind.

Will you forgive me for offering myself as an example on this altar of homiletical sacrifice? I have enjoyed preaching and writing, but I remember, with a shame which still smarts, the too frequent occasions, both in speech and print, when I have been found out wrong as to facts. I can recall the men who justly criticized me, the times and places of their criticism, and the passages which warranted it. The mistakes were trivial matters—wrong names, and dates, and quotations—but they were not allowed to pass unchallenged. To be caught neatly between bases and thrown out on a matter of fact is a humiliating experience.

Furthermore, I have learned, after ten or fifteen years of preaching in a university chapel, that one had better not parade a little knowledge in the presence of persons who have much knowledge. For example, a college preacher is not well advised to dwell upon the spiritual significance of the new physics if he has, as may well happen, a Nobel prize-winner in that field sitting in the fourth pew from the front. I find that in such presence it is the part of discretion not to draw romantic Christian lessons from the works of Jeans and Eddington, tempting as the prospect is. One may be warranted in quoting verbatim what modern physicists are saying; one is less warranted in telling them how fully Christian they are without knowing it. It is quite conceivable that Einstein also is among the prophets, but if so he should be allowed to announce the fact himself. The same reticence is advisable in our references to astronomy, mathematics, history, art, and the new psychology. Since the Professor of Psychiatry in the Harvard Medical School, whom I am happy to count a personal friend, is one of the regular attendants at our Sunday morning service, I do not lightly mention the theories of Freud, Adler, and Jung. I try to cite such matters discreetly and advisedly. These more rigorous habits have had to be developed in self-defence. The discipline has been severe, but it has been salutary, and I am grateful for it. The necessity of preaching from matters of fact on which I may be supposed to have reasonable knowledge has been of itself one insight into the nature of our task. My observation is that the professors in the pews are more interested in what I can tell them about the Bible than in my attempts to teach them their own subjects.

You will say that the college preacher is an unfortunately placed exception to what is otherwise a kindlier rule. I doubt it. The faculty members of his congregation set a standard in their class-rooms which their students carry away into the outside world. These same students may slough off in college their outgrown theologies, but they learn there new tempers which are both moral and spiritual—accuracy, honesty, sincerity. One way to keep our college students in church when they come back is to greet them with a mind which does not need to make concessions to the precision of the class-rooms they learned to love and respect.

Furthermore, it is bad for a man himself to feel that he can go on playing fast and loose with facts, trading upon the ignorance of his congregation. Perhaps the pews will not identify your errors, but it is becoming increasingly unsafe to rest your reputation as a man of learning upon the illiteracy of your hearers. More people know about more things than ever before. Such prudential considerations are, however, beside the mark. The real issue is that of the preacher's own integrity. A man who stands in a pulpit and speaks from it ought not to lack confidence in the processes of his own thinking. Chronic carelessness must in the end rot his mind, and he will degenerate into a pedlar of platitudes or a vendor of rhetoric.

The specific forms of our professional indifference to fact should be kept in mind as we make and preach sermons. There is the failure to assemble a sufficient body of assured fact to warrant our superstructure of idealism. Most of us work hurriedly and carelessly here. Far too many of our Utopias hang in mid-air. They lack precisely that quality of initial sobriety which we can identify in the Jewish Messianic hope, which drew its best metaphors from the actual world at hand.

Then there is our partisan habit of picking and choosing only such facts as tell for the case we are trying to make, and deliberately neglecting those which tell in other directions. This is a common human error. I have always remembered with amusement a parishioner who was during the war a militarist of the most romantic type. Feeling that I was imperfectly attuned to the situation, she came to me one day with an article she had clipped from some paper. She said, "I have read two pieces lately about soldiers, both written by religious workers with the army. One says that our soldiers are pure and noble; the other says that they are a rough lot. I threw the second article into the wastebasket and cut out the first one for you to read!" The pews are not the only sinners after this kind. We preachers too often wittingly throw into the waste basket inconvenient facts. We consciously withhold damaging evidence against our case. We tell the truth, but not the whole truth. A preacher should be just to the other side. A lack of intellectual generosity and of fair-mindedness will, in the end, undermine his influence.

Again, there is the shabby habit of introducing into a sermon facts which we have not mastered. We all do this. At our best we do it because we believe that in the prodigal welter of contemporary thought he who is not against us is for us, and hold ourselves entitled to enlist on our side any one who has not professed himself hostile to it. Meanwhile we are yielding to the temptation to surround ourselves with a glamour of cosmopolitanism, by creating a reputation for knowing our way around the modern world of ideas. We appear as cronies of the talked-about thinkers and writers of the day. But one of the best five-minute addresses I have heard at morning prayers in the Harvard Chapel was given by a Professor of Greek, on the verse in I Corinthians, "For I determined not to know anything among you, save Jesus Christ, and him crucified." These words of Saint Paul's, he said, are unintelligible until set against the background of the speech before the Areopagus, in which the apostle had tried to parade his knowledge of Greek poetry and Greek philosophy with signal want of success. After that futile experience, Saint Paul decided to talk on matters of which he had first-hand experience and knowledge. Whether the exegesis be correct or not, the point is well taken. You and I are much too prone to bring into our sermons the involved theories of scientists, the speculations of philosophers, passages from the classics, references to historical movements, on which we should much prefer not to be examined in further detail.

Such, then, are the sins of indifference to fact which do so easily beset us. We must keep vigil against them. We should do well to go to school to that single law of letters which Scott, the editor of the *Manchester Guardian*, imposed upon both his leader writers and his reporters: "Opinions are free; but facts are sacred."

What, then, of the specific skills which we ought to master; skills which, when mastered, will enable us to hold up our heads with good conscience and a proper professional self-respect among our fellows in the world at large? They are, I think, three.

A minister should be skilled in a knowledge of human nature. He should be fully a man and should count nothing human foreign to himself. He should be one who needs not that any testify to him of man, for he knows what is in man. This skill alone might cost a lifetime of discipline. Yet it cannot ever quite be gained by study. It is in equal part a grace which comes to us through a native sympathy and imagination. Without a fellow-feeling for your human kind, no text books in psychology can ever give it to you. The world has a right to expect, when it turns to the minister of religion, that it will meet in him one who understands in advance the secrets which it comes to confess, the perplexities on which it asks advice, the temptations with which it wrestles, the sorrows which burden its heart, the hopes which it can never quite relinquish. What men are, and do, and bear, if not the only study of the minister, is always his proper study. Without an insight into human nature, compounded of our own first-hand experience of life, of our observation of other men, and of our deepening knowledge of the world's classics, we stand condemned as unskilled workmen in our profession.

A minister should be skilled in ceremonial. The great occasions of life, whether they be private or public, call for recognition and formal expression. To let them pass uncelebrated, or to celebrate them inadequately, is felt to be a grievous error. A marriage performed by a justice of the peace satisfies the requirements of the civil law, but such a ceremony is a meagre symbol of the mysterious transaction in process. The instinct which demands " a church wedding" is more than a desire for the social decencies. The secular prose of things falls short of our major joys and sorrows, our festivals and anniversary times. Man cries out for poetry, and ceremonial is the answer of the race to this cry. Every community needs men who can care for life's proper poetry—what Cardinal Newman once called its "legitimate rhetoric."

Needing such men, the community is entitled to persons in whom it can have confidence. It is not enough in this life to be able to trust the engineers who build our skyscrapers and all those whom they typify. We must also have artists whom we can trust. It is a happy thing for us that when we go to the symphony we do not have to worry lest Toscanini lose his place or Myra Hess forget her sonata. Not only so, but the minimal standard we require at a symphony concert is high. We do not expect the third clarinetist to play a wrong note, or the drummer to beat his percussion during a rest. We abandon all such anxieties and yield ourselves confidently to the tide of the music. When men and women come to church they ought to come with the confidence that no carelessness, no ignorance, no violations of taste on our part shall get between them and their desire to be led in acts of devotion. In particular we should be able to find fit words through which men may pray. There are many of us in the ministry today who are more concerned for the prayers in a service than for its sermon. If we could learn better how to pray and teach others how to pray we should have done the world what is perhaps our greatest single professional service. We should then be truly skilled in the conduct of public worship.

And, finally, our third skill is that of preaching. It is the one by which we shall always be most

easily identified and most commonly appraised. I
suppose the most familiar judgment passed upon
us runs thus: "No, he is not very much of a
preacher, but . . . he does thus and so pretty well."
The initial qualification identifies the yardstick by
which we are first measured. The traditional discipline of preaching calls for all the wit and learning and ingenuity we have. Occasionally a sermon
can be preached quite extemporaneously. Yet I
doubt whether such extemporaneity is as much a
thing of the moment as it seems. Behind the power
to say things well without immediate preparation
lie the years we have spent in giving thought to religion and our discipline in putting words together.
Five thousand dollars is a tremendous fee to pay
a surgeon for forty minutes' work. But there are
some surgeons sought after in difficult cases who
are not overpaid if they get that figure. You are
not paying them for forty minutes; if you pay them
at all you are paying them for the knowledge of a
lifetime. All such figures are arbitrary. Our best
sermons are written quickly, left alone, and
preached without revision. How long did it take
us to write them? Three hours, possibly four or
five? No, it took us all our lives to write those sermons. The longer actual time taken for the prepa-

ration of sermons not so good is in reality much shorter.

You know, when you hear a man speak, whether there is steady thinking, an independent life of the mind, behind his words. You know whether he has worked patiently and doggedly at the ways of saying things. He cannot deceive you. Whatever else you may think of his sermon—and it does not matter whether you agree with his ideas or not— you respect him as a person fit to live and work in our modern world, if he convinces you that he is a man of discipline and skill. This moral confidence in a preacher's craftsmanship means more to you than agreement with his theology, because his craftsmanship is a clue to his character. In this unintelligible world, we trust and respect a great many men with whom we sharply disagree. Merely to find yourself agreeing with a speaker whose words betray a want of professional good conscience in their preparation is a hollow satisfaction.

In one of his essays, George Macaulay Trevelyan says:

The idea that histories which are delightful to read must be the work of superficial temperaments, and that a crabbed style betokens a deep thinker or conscientious worker, is the reverse of the truth. What is easy to read has been difficult to write. The labour of writing and rewriting, correcting and recorrecting, is the due exacted by every good book from its author, even if he knows from the beginning exactly what he wants to say. A limpid style is invariably the result of hard labour, and the easily flowing connection of sentence with sentence has always been won by the sweat of the brow.[2]

Those words may be paraphrased with reference to sermons. The theory that a sermon which we find it easy to hear has been easy to prepare is false. The sermons which are easily prepared are usually heard with difficulty and only half understood. What the man in the pew finds easy to hear has been hard to plan and write and say.

Preaching is the most characteristic and individual of our public acts. It is, in the main, the one by which we stand or fall before the community. We shall not win the battle elsewhere if we neglect it here. I do not mean that we can all be great preachers or even very good preachers. I do mean that when we stand before people to speak to them in God's behalf, we should do so with a clear conscience. Careless preaching, more potently than any other professional defect, will disqualify us for membership in a society which is already familiar with the meaning of the words, discipline and skill. To lead the world at large to suspect that at this

[2] *Clio, a Muse.* George Macaulay Trevelyan; Longmans, Green and Co., London, 1914, p. 34.

crucial point you are an undisciplined person, and to demonstrate to your congregation Sunday by Sunday your lack of skill, is not merely to close the doors against yourself in the future, it is to widen still further the already ominous gulf between the skilled professions and trades on the one hand and an unskilled ministry on the other. You owe it to the cause, as well as to yourself, to give the community moral confidence in you as a preacher, even though your hearers may disagree with you in many details of both your theology and your ethics. Given the traditional tempers of Protestantism, the pulpit is the place where we shall recover or forfeit still further our right to live among our peers in the world of today. A preacher should be "a workman that needeth not to be ashamed." To go into a pulpit year after year with a professionally bad conscience about one's sermons is to exile oneself from the society of serious and skilled men.

CHAPTER VII

The Timeliness of Our Sermons

EVERY man born into the world thinks of himself as a late-comer in time. His belatedness seems to him an absolute rather than a relative fact. His conviction finds a classical statement in the metaphor of the reaper who enters a field which has already been harvested.

Choirilos of Samos, a Greek poet of the fifth century B.C., writes, "Happy the man who was skilled in song, a servant of the Muses at the time when the meadow was virgin. But now, when all things have been divided up and the arts have their bounds, we are left as it were late in the race, and it is not possible to drive a new chariot." Two hundred years before our era Ben Sirach said of himself, "I awaked up last of all, as one that gathereth after the grape-gatherers." Fifteen hundred years later, in fourteenth-century England, we find Chaucer using the same figure:

> For wel I wot that ye han her-biforn
> Of making ropen, and lad away the corn;

And I come after, glening here and there,
And am ful glad if I may find an ere
Of any goodly word that ye han left.

What is the cause of this stubborn persuasion
that the world is growing old? Why are men forever saying, "Little children, it is the last time?"
The question takes on a new urgency for us because of the conviction, already a commonplace in
Europe and fast becoming plausible here, that we
who are now alive are living at the end of an age.

Obviously, the idea must have at least a psychological warrant, otherwise it could not have survived so many repeated rebuffs at the hand of the
event. Each of the three writers whom we quoted
a moment ago, so far from living in the last times,
was looking out upon the freshness of an early
world. Why, then, did each hold so strongly to the
idea that he incarnated the world's old age? Does
each oncoming, inexpert age gain needed self-con-
fidence by affecting, as youth is prone to do, sophistication and world-weariness? Does each new-born
generation leap from the knowledge that it is the
latest arrival on the scene to the inference that it is
therefore to be the last arrival? Is this idea necessitated by the patent contrast between the certain
past and the uncertain future? It is hard to say.

Most of us modernists had supposed that eschatologies and apocalypses were things of the theological past. The gospels contain inconvenient material which falls within these schemes, but we had made our peace with that problem. We should have preferred to believe that Jesus never made use of such ideas, and that material to this effect in the synoptic gospels was foisted upon him by the editors. In so far as critical honesty forbade this comfortable conclusion, we accepted the alternative and admitted that he probably thought and taught within the apocalyptic framework. If so, he was, after all, what we would wish him to have been—a man of his own time. His inability to anticipate the doctrine of a gradual historical evolution is proof of his perfect humanity. Such were our reflections on what seemed to us little less than a blemish on the serene pages of the gospels.

We are now confronted with the possibility that Jesus—the Jesus of Schweitzer—may have been more nearly right than we supposed; right at least in his instinct for the way things happen in time, if not in actual detail; right in historical spirit, if not in the historical letter. Such, for example, is the conclusion reached by Berdyaev. He says:

The tie between Christianity and history is such as exists in no other world religion. The philosophy of history is in its origins intimately allied to eschatology; and this helps to explain its rise among the Jewish people. Eschatology is the doctrine of the goal of history. It presupposes a catastrophic fulfilment which inaugurates a new world and a new reality.[1]

The revolutions of our time are to Berdyaev vindications of his thesis. Himself a victim of the Russian revolution, he is willing to concede that that revolution could never have happened in want of the deep feeling for destiny, and of a faith in catastrophic fulfilments of destiny, which is the essence of the Christian world view. Karl Marx, he tells us, stands in a lineal descent which derives direct from the prophecy of Daniel through the book of the Revelation. Having little heart for the forms of Soviet life, Berdyaev can still see in them perverse expressions of the traditional Christian philosophy of history.

Meanwhile the letter of this stubborn faith in the catastrophic happening, which is to bring about the end of the age, has suffered certain changes. In its primitive Jewish-Christian form, the doctrine anticipated a final divine intervention in human affairs. Things were to go from bad to worse till God ended them all. God will endure the world as long as he can, then he will flood it with his righteous wrath and a new age will begin. It is

[1] *The Meaning of History*, Nicholas Berdyaev. New York: Charles Scribner's Sons, 1936, pp. 32, 33, 34.

most significant that in some such expectation the natural sciences of the nineteenth century were wholly orthodox. So far from discarding the Christian eschatologies and apocalypses, they merely rehabilitated them in secular forms. Science foresees a day when life will no longer be possible on this planet. We shall be scorched out in collision with some wandering star, or we shall be frozen out between walls of ice returning from the poles. Rhetorical descriptions of the end of the world are to be found in sober books of modern astronomy or physics, more terrible than anything foretold in Daniel and Revelation, because more probable. The fact that all this is to happen at some far distant time does not, for thoughtful men, make the end less sombre. If the universe is eventually to foreclose its mortgage on this planet, there is little use trying to improve our petty cash balances in the meantime. Our duty, as Spengler says, is to hold without hope a position which is already as good as lost.

At present, however, eschatological and apocalyptic dogmas are taking on a fresh lease of life in another and even more sinister form. You must often have noticed that what you supposed was an account of events in outer nature and history turns out to be a description of your own inner life. It is by no means clear what inferences are to be drawn from this experience; they seem to point in the direction of a subjective account of reality. Meanwhile the experience is a common one, recalling that striking verse in the books of Acts, which introduces the "we" section. A story, which until then had been told in the third person, must hereafter be told, with all the added weight and intensity given by the shift of subject, in the first person.

Some such change has come over our thought of the end of the world. The agent of our destruction, if destruction is to come, will not be the wrath of God, nor a thrice-heated star, nor glacial ice; it will be ourselves. Modern man as a political animal is hag-ridden by the fear that he may commit corporate suicide. He knows he ought not to harbor such ideas. He realizes that such a thought is in itself a symptom of insanity. He is, however, a pathological person in the grip of a dread which he cannot throw off. How far, how very far, we have come from the bland premises of liberalism which, a half century ago, assured us that whatever else might be true, this was true—we had cast fear out of our minds! There can never have been a time in the world's history when more people were desperately afraid than at this present time—afraid of one another and of themselves.

Individual men not only think about suicide and cunningly plan it; they commit it. Furthermore, the doctors tell us that talking about suicide does not provide the necessary safety valve, for many persons who talk about taking their own lives end by doing so. They are not in normal mental health, but sanity is a thing of precarious balance and hard to restore once it has been unsettled. If there be any correspondence between the life of the individual and the life of society, there would seem to be no reason why whole communities should not become infected by the idea of suicide, and turn their morbid fancies into tragic fact. I must confess that this is the only explanation I can find for many of the tempers which are now abroad in Europe.

We have here one possible explanation of the baffling sense of futility and defeatism which attends most of our efforts for world peace. The pacifist program has always assumed that you could appeal to a man's reason, and at its daring best has believed that you could evoke his capacity for Christian love. The common sense argument for world peace rests the case upon enlightened self-interest. On paper, and even in fact, its logic seems incontrovertible. No sane man now supposes that it is economically possible to win a war. All are losers together, and the world as a whole is so much the poorer. As for religious pacifism, the non-resistant gospel of love assumes that there is at the bottom of the human soul a residual goodness which will recognize the refusal to meet blow with blow as a creative attitude, and will throw down its arms in response to that appeal. We have supposed that non-resistance would work, and as strategy it has been seriously commended as more likely to work than any other method to which we can have recourse.

These suppositions seem less likely to be true at present than at any time in recent history. They are, without any question of a doubt, much less plausible than they were in 1914. All pleas for peace addressed to economic self-interest, as the good of each secured by the common good of all together, seem to fall on deaf ears in the danger spots of modern Europe. One cannot conceive that either Germany or Italy in their present frame of mind will be deterred for a day from going ahead with their programs by any considerations addressed by the world at large to our total economic well-being. Likewise, we must not assume that Russia is the sort of country of which Tolstoi dreamed. The present regime has committed itself, wisely from its own standpoint, to consolidating its position at home before attempting to spread the gospel abroad. But he is a fool who thinks that Russian communism has any necessary or permanent affinities with pacifism.

As to the idealistic, non-resistant appeal, it is wholly conceivable that an increasing number of Christians may conclude that this is the only decent moral response left to the military menace of our times. The world may have gone so far down the path to destruction that the best we can do is to let men take our lives if they so wish and will. But we have not the slightest warrant for supposing that non-resistance will succeed as a counsel of worldly prudence. Persons holding this view must not be surprised if, in the terms of present life, the method does not work. They must be prepared to see their countries taken and their cultures destroyed, even though they be left alive to walk in chains behind the chariot of their conquerors. The kingdom to which the non-resistant belongs is today not of this world; I doubt if it ever was.

Some such prospect seems more certain than at any time within living memory, for the simple reason that a common-sense view of the prohibitory economic cost of war, and a Christian view of the sinfulness of war, waken no echoes in the minds which are the danger spots. Either one of two things is true: either the new ideologies have wholly dispossessed common sense and Christianity, or else we are dealing with <u>pathological minds which, by</u> <u>reason of mental strain, are immune</u> to rationality <u>and religion.</u> It is not an extreme statement of our situation to say that we shall be most closely geared to our job as peacemakers if we proceed on the assumption that in these matters we are dealing with persons who are suffering from delusions of grandeur and are dangerous with the danger that insanity brings. If it be said that there still must be in these countries serene and Christian souls untouched by madness, we can only say that they have not yet succeeded in modifying the direction of events taken by their leaders. To this general thesis the gallant stand of the Confessional Churches in Germany is the one signal exception. We are prompted to help such minorities, but help from the outside is more often a liability than an asset, and from persons so placed we have more than once had requests that we do not make ourselves too vocal in their behalf. We only complicate their problem. The Wilson strategy of appealing over the heads of the rulers to the common people is less likely to work now than it was twenty years ago.

If some such account of the strange sense of a helplessness which has come over the peace movement does not satisfy you, you are under bonds to produce a better. For myself, I have come slowly to the conclusion that we must realize that in many nations we are dealing with a radically diseased mind, which at times seems to take on the form of a suicidal mania. Our problem is quite as much medical as it is economic and ethical. If I were asked to defend this imputation of corporate insanity to whole societies of persons, I should say that the loss of the right to self-criticism and the power of self-criticism is proof of the fact. A madman cannot criticize himself. The criterion of sanity is the willingness to admit that other people may be right and you may be wrong.

Today there is no such thing left in our world as immunity to ideas. Infections and contagions take place across all borders. For three centuries the happenings of Europe have had a way of being re-enacted in America. Such is the profit and such is the penalty we pay for our diverse origins in the Old World. Nothing is more likely than that we shall see in this country re-enactments of the drama being worked out in Europe. The catch-words and the names are already a commonplace among us, and are bandied back and forth as terms of praise and blame applied to our own affairs. The words take on a deadly seriousness precisely because they represent ideologies, a far more terrible reality than the native yelp of the animal man. You can

tame a brute in time; it is hard to convert a doctrinaire philosopher. Such, then, is the world to
which we are likely to be preaching in the years
immediately ahead.

Now, a sermon is not a succession of sentences
launched aimlessly into the void. It is a compound
of words addressed directly to living men and
women where they are and as they are. Not all the
truths of religion are relevant all the time. The
effectiveness of a sermon depends very largely
upon a timeliness and pertinence which are achieved
without sacrifice of inherent truthfulness. Professor
Whitehead says in one of his recent books, "I
hazard the prophecy that that religion will conquer
which can render clear to popular understanding
some eternal greatness in the passage of temporal
fact."[2] We could have no better account of the way
in which today we may become more than conquerors through preaching.

It is easy enough to stand in a pulpit and announce what you regard as eternal truth, without
reference to its fitness to the needs of the world
before you. One remembers the story of a well-
meaning tract distributor who passed over the field
of Gettysburg on the evening after the battle, hand-

[2] *Adventures of Ideas*, Alfred North Whitehead, New York:
The Macmillan Company, 1933, p. 41.

ing out his wares with a fine impartiality, and putting into the hands of one poor soldier, whose legs had been mangled by a shell, a treatise on the evils of dancing. Such catholic indiscriminateness does not satisfy the ideal of the sermon. There is a time for every truth of religion, and not all times are the same. To announce impersonally and dispassionately what are called eternal truths is not good preaching. Such practice, in public and in the pulpit, partakes too much of ascetic detachment from the world.

Nor is it enough to be merely a reporter. For a long time now there have been lodged in my mind two grim sentences which Mr. H. G. Wells wrote in the London *Nation* for the third week of August, 1914. For years he had been foretelling the oncoming European war. No one had paid any attention to him. If people heard what he tried to tell them they said, as their predecessors had said to another pessimist long before, "The vision that he seeth is for many days to come, and he prophesieth of the times that are far off." Then the war came and Mr. Wells replied: "I am not writing prophecies now, and I am not 'displaying imagination.' I am running as hard as I can beside the marching facts and pointing at them."[3] His words

[3] *The Nation* (London), August 15, 1914, p. 733.

seemed to me nakedly true then, and they have
become more true with each passing day. I know
of no better account of our mental history over
the last twenty-five years. We have been running
as hard as we can beside fast-marching facts, and
pointing at them. A kind of mental breathlessness
is abroad, which is reflected in the art of our time.
The dramas and the novels which are the most
faithful transcript of our lives record, on the sensitive film of consciousness, the hurrying events of
the outer world. What the events mean, whether
they have any rhyme or reason, we cannot stop to
ask. It is important to take the mental picture
while the action is going on, because it will not be
re-enacted. We must keep turning the crank of the
camera; we can study the film later at our leisure,
running it at slow speed to see what it has to tell.
You may, if you choose to do so, make a popular
success of your ministry by joining the horde of
competent reporters and movie men who are re-
cording what is now happening. People are interested in the march of time and are willing to listen
to its broadcast. But this again does not satisfy the
ideal of the sermon. A Christian preacher is not
one more reporter or photographer. He is not
engrossed in the business of making films either for
the interest of his contemporaries or for study by

posterity. He is, in Professor Whitehead's words, trying to help men and women find some eternal greatness in the passage of temporal facts.

What is the American preacher to make of it all, and say to it all? I can only tell you what one man thinks of it, and bid you confirm or correct his impression by yours. No political revolution is the end of the world in the sense in which the writers of Jewish apocalypses conceived of that event. We are apt to under-rate the human will-to-live. Nothing that has ever happened in history has permanently interrupted man's elemental concerns —his hunger for bread, his tilling of the soil, his love of woman, the begetting of the unborn generation yet to come, and his innate belief in life. In the fourth book of *The Prelude*, Wordsworth describes a dream in which he saw the world coming to an end before his eyes. When he wakened he reflected on the dream and wrote:

A thought is with me sometimes, and I say,
Should earth by inward throes be wrench'd throughout,
Or fire be sent from far to wither all
Her pleasant habitations, and dry up
Old Ocean in his bed left sing'd and bare,
Yet would the living Presence still subsist
Victorious; and a composure would ensue,
And kindlings like the morning; presage sure,
Though slow, perhaps, of a returning day.

The transactions of human life are forever taking place at two levels: a surface level where culture, civilization, statecraft, the applied sciences, the organization of labor, the arbitrary fixing of the worth of money concern us greatly; and a deeper level, a kind of subsoil, which remains much the same whatever the surface changes, where there are birth and death, love and play and art. Prophetic religion is always actively concerned with the changes of life at the surface; but it loses its religious quality and becomes merely social reform if it ceases to draw its nourishment from the subsoil of man's constant experiences. The book of Job and the Beatitudes will be true in every culture which we can foresee, and there will always be need of them. Short of all that we mean by heaven, they can never be outgrown; no political or economic revolution can out-mode them. Meanwhile, since the visible changes of contemporary history are rapid, revolutionary, and all-absorbing in their interest, we cannot as preachers ignore them. What is our present expectation of life at this level, and what eternal greatness can we discover in passing events?

Europe is apparently being drawn slowly toward the "next war." That war, if it comes, will be a struggle between Fascism-*cum*-Nazism, "the Rome-Berlin axis" and the Russian Soviets. There seems to be little old-fashioned capitalism left in Italy and Germany, and equally little ideal communism as yet realized in Russia. In all these states a drastic form of state socialism is in force, and, so far as the lot of the private citizen is concerned, he and his fortunes are at the mercy of the state. Where the rights of the individual are concerned there is much less to choose between these rival systems than is commonly suggested.

We cannot resist the conclusion that if Christianity is to endure and in due time to overcome the world, it will find in retrospect that it had, during the first half of the twentieth century, more in common with Russia than with Germany and Italy, solely because the former aspired to a catholic faith while the latter were determined to perpetuate denominational faiths. We cling, and cling rightly, to any scheme for the organization of human life which invokes super-nationalism rather than nationalism.

But unless we think that the full requirements of our religion are met in the prosecution of the class war and the drastic redistribution of this world's goods, we shall not allow a purely doctrinaire interest in Communism to lead us to sell our Christian birthright to Stalin. We hear much of the religious genius of communism. It may be a religion, but it is a religion of the most primitive sort. Despite its grasp of what may prove to be one of the determining ideas in economic history hereafter, Russian Communism is at present a barbarous and savage cult which, so far from advancing the clock of spiritual religion, is setting it back to the ages of inquisition, torture, unthinkable cruelties, and human sacrifice. It is a religion in the same sense in which the fanaticisms, bigotries, and bloodsheds of the past have been religion. It is the religion of the Mad Mullah or the mediaeval Mohammedan. It is, if you will, the lusty and lawless religion of the Crusades. To say that men will live sacrificial lives for it and die for it, is not to make a place for it among those maturer tempers of the human spirit, to which we thought we had worked our way, out of the slaughter houses of the past. It can become a catholic religion only by butchering or subjugating all its foes, since it seeks no comradeship and recognizes no kinship with those who do not share its class consciousness and implacable class hatreds. Let us admit that it is a religion, but let us not cease to remember what kind of religion it is—precisely that kind of religion which the best elements in the human spirit have for centuries been struggling to supersede. These considerations stand

quite apart from its insights into the probable re-
organization of industry and redistribution of
wealth, and concern the temper with which its
faith is professed, enforced, and spread. However
much we may agree with its foreshadowing of
changes which are already in process the world
over, there would be no place for you and me, or
any of our kind, within its present fabric. We should
be, in the terms of our present life, out of a job,
refugees elsewhere, or dead.

Meanwhile it is an error of fact to assume that
the whole history of contemporary Europe is exhausted by the antithesis between German and
Italian ambitions on the one hand, and Russian
intentions on the other. That this is the centre of
interest at the present time, and the spot of danger,
no one will deny. What the world calls "news"
comes from this source. But the development of
the totalitarian idea in the states which have now
espoused it has had in certain European countries,
particularly in England and France, the effect of
fortifying faith in democratic institutions and of
rehabilitating to some degree the supposedly discredited liberalism of a generation ago. Germany
and Italy have their active sympathizers in England and France. These are, however, in the minority, and only the naked necessity of guaranteeing

the perpetuity of national life would incline either England or France to cast their military lot with the one side and against the other. The soberer minds in the surviving democracies of Europe are saying to the rival systems on the Continent, with increased impatience and conviction, "A plague on both your houses." The assumption that democracy is dead and liberalism a spent force is premature. The Labor Party in England has formally refused to associate or identify itself with official communism. The parlor radical is less pink than he was five years ago. Altogether, the present moment sees an increasing unwillingness of the non-Nazi, non-Fascist, non-Soviet states of Europe to be involved as partisans in the "next war."

We are Americans. We have culturally fewer near-of-kin left in the Old World than we had a generation ago—in England certainly, in the Scandinavian countries surely, in Belgium and Switzerland possibly, in France probably. Otherwise the culture which we have developed over three centuries is imperilled in Europe. We have listlessly agreed to the assumption that that culture is passing here, and there is no doubt of the radical changes taking place in American life. No political party can stop them. The America of the future will be a land of fewer unhappy contrasts than the America of the past. We have in the last few years written into our laws many provisions for social well-being which were long overdue. However they may be modified in form, they will not be deleted in substance, and others of like nature will follow. The thrust of life is in that direction.

The spiritual problem which we face is a relatively simple one—whether the hard-won and still precious virtue of religious liberalism has any further worth among us, or only a sale price. If the latter, it must go the way it has gone in many of the countries of the Old World. In going, it will carry with it all that the Reformation fought for and all that Protestantism ideally still stands for— the right of private conscience. The forces most potently and ominously at work in Europe have no place for the nonconforming individual, for dissenting minorities, or for personal faith at variance with national dogma.

These considerations raise the question whether we have any right, much less a duty, to allow the spiritual values of our national life to be caught between the upper and nether millstones of the coming Fascist-Communist struggle and scattered as dust to the wind. Conservative and institutionally minded persons will tend to sympathize with the one side; impatient and impulsive natures with the other. But is anything serviceable to our world, for any future which we can forecast, to be gained by partisanships which, in either direction, disallow the heritage and culture which are ours?

Religion is for most of us a desperate struggle for something like an accurate perspective. Such imperfect perspective as we have tentatively achieved is now in danger of being wiped out by uncritical and impetuous sympathies with one or another of the two European protagonists. Liberal religion in particular is a type of spiritual life in which the power of self-criticism is highly developed. This is, as I have indicated earlier, a quality peculiar to Christian prophetism. We have not been wholly wanting in that mature virtue. We have for a half century been ill at ease about the state of our churches, the unequal distribution of our wealth, the condition of our industrial laborers, the lot of our prisoners, the tragedy of the Negro, the corruption of our courts. These facts have been our meat and drink, day and night. They have lain heavy on our conscience, and we have worked patiently for their bettering. We have, therefore, no right, much less no call, to throw away in one random gesture our hard-won sense of perspective by suggesting that life here is pretty much what it is in Russia or Germany or Italy. There is a point beyond which overstatement defeats itself. The Scottsboro boys may serve a life sentence, but if so, it will not be without an honest attempt made by many public-spirited persons to find the truth and to save them if they are innocent. In those other lands thousands upon thousands of innocent persons have gone down the wind that blows between the worlds, and no whisper of social self-criticism within the scheme has been heard in their behalf. The two things are of different dimensions and happen within different frameworks; the one within a confessedly imperfect and often frustrated liberalism, the other within a brutal illiberality.

There is grave danger lest, living through at a distance the oncoming struggle in the Old World, we shall allow our fears, or our prudence, or our heady idealism to deprive us of that hard-won perspective in religion which sees in the power of self-criticism one of the most precious achievements of the more recent centuries of our religion. We can easily forfeit, in a few hours of panic or hot-headed enthusiasm, all that Protestantism has been groping after for four hundred years—a temper and way of the spiritual life rather than any single dogma, theological, political, or economic. I cannot believe that we are now ready to renounce that Protestantism which, in some ways, has been given its freest field in our own land. It remains, if not the only one, at least one, of the possible saving forces of the future.

Those of us who stand in the Protestant tradition have been listening patiently for years to wholesale criticisms of our interpretation of the Christian life. We have been told that Protestantism is to blame for nationalism and for capitalism, with all the abuses that have lived under their joint aegis. We have heard that our individualistic religion has delayed indefinitely a truly social order. We have become accustomed to playing the scapegoat for the world's waning faith in God and its loss of religion, because our attention has been centered too much, perhaps, upon man. We do not deny the grounds for these charges, and more often than otherwise have bowed our heads in silent consent. Clearly we Protestants have not yet led our world out of its wilderness wanderings into the promised land. The duty of self-examination is laid upon us with fresh urgency. Whatever is written in serious criticism of us we must read earnestly.

But I come back to my axiom, that religion is a struggle for perspective. Therefore we have no business to be diverted from our own proper spiritual concerns and lured back into ancient obscurantisms. The reactionary theologies of Europe most to the front at the present time are counsels of despair. We can understand why tired and disillusioned men have fallen back on them, but that is no reason why we should believe them. The most sober judges in our field whom I know foretell a time of superstition, sentimentalism, and wilful dogmatism in religion. Whatever the inherent defects of our interpretation of Christianity, and whatever our failures in action, we have no right to lay upon the future any heavier burden than it will have to bear when it receives from the present reactionary age its heritage of spiritual counsels darkened by a contempt for knowledge. This is not an occasion for Protestant self-congratulation; it is a matter of our debt to the cause. There can be no permanent future hope for Christian thought in the theological retreats which are being sounded all along the line. We may agree with everything that the cavalier critic of Protestantism has to say of its achievements thus far: nevertheless, our kind of religion holds at least one of the bridgeheads by which anything which we recognize as historic Christianity can pass over into the future. Our problem is how to concede every valid criticism and to preserve our power of self-criticism, without abandoning altogether the position which four hundred years of history assign to us.

I was much struck and deeply moved the other day on hearing a member of the Society of Friends speak upon these things. He is a man in mature life, whose conscience is acutely sensitive and who has more than once suffered at the hands of the existing order. He said, in substance, "Until most recently I have always felt that the man with a streak of the fanatic in him is the true exponent of religion. But as I look around my world today, I find myself questioning whether I have been right. For it seems to me that the fanatical temper, with its necessary strain of passionate self-righteousness, is beginning to cost our world too dear. To my surprise, I have found myself wondering whether, from the standpoint of the purest religion, the spirit of tolerance is not even greater, whether it is not at the present time the one Christian temper most needed in our world."

We began our first lecture with a reference to Jeremy Taylor's *Discourse of the Liberty of Prophesying*, and now, at the end of our last lecture, we can do no better than return to it.

This great *Discourse* is a brief for tolerance. It was written in a time when intolerance was abroad, but it did not fall victim to its own day.

Its survival should persuade us that the patient and generous tempers of the Christian religion have in them more promise of life than is generated by ungracious controversy. Why is it, asks Jeremy Taylor, that men impose upon one another, intellectually and morally? This habit, he replies, "came as other abuses and corruptions did, by reason of the iniquity of the times, and the cooling of the first heats of Christianity, and the abatements of Christian simplicity. . . . It is not the differing opinions that is the cause of the present ruptures, but want of Charity. . . . All these mischiefs proceed not from this, that men are not of one mind, for that is neither necessary nor possible, but that every Opinion is made an Article of Faith, every Article is a group of a quarrel, every quarrel makes a faction, every faction is zealous, and all zeal pretends for God, and whatsoever is for God cannot be too much; we by this time are come to that pass, we think we love not God unless we persecute all religions but our own."

If there was ever an age that needed the gracious spirit which inspired the *Discourse of the Liberty of Prophesying*, it is our own age, already so rent with recriminations and so menaced by misunderstandings. Let the last word of these lectures be Jeremy Taylor's: "In this world we believe in part, and prophesy in part, and this imperfection shall never be done away, till we be translated to a more glorious state: either then we must throw our chances, and get truth by accident or predestination, or else we must lie safe in an imperial toleration, and private liberty of persuasion, unless some other method can be thought upon, where we may fasten our floating vessels, and ride safely."

THE LYMAN BEECHER LECTURES ON
PREACHING

YALE UNIVERSITY
Established May 2, 1872

1871-72 Henry Ward Beecher, *Yale Lectures on Preaching*, first series.
N. Y., J. B. Ford & Co., 1872.

1872-73 Henry Ward Beecher, *Yale Lectures on Preaching*, second series.
N. Y., J. B. Ford & Co., 1873.

1873-74 Henry Ward Beecher, *Yale Lectures on Preaching*, third series.
N. Y., J. B. Ford & Co., 1874.

1874-75 John Hall, *God's Word Through Preaching*.
N. Y., Dodd & Mead, 1875.

1875-76 William Mackergo Taylor, *The Ministry of the Word*.
N. Y., Anson D. F. Randolph & Co., 1876.

1876-77 Phillips Brooks, *Lectures on Preaching*.
N. Y., E. P. Dutton, 1877.

1877-78 Robert William Dale, *Nine Lectures on Preaching*.
N. Y., A. S. Barnes & Co., 1878.

1878-79 Matthew Simpson, *Lectures on Preaching*.
N. Y., Nelson & Phillips, 1879.

1879-80   Howard Crosby, *The Christian Preacher*.
       N. Y., Anson D. F. Randolph, 1880.

1880-81   Joseph Tuthill Duryea, Title not known.
       Lectures unpublished.

1881-82   Ezekiel Gilman Robinson, *Lectures on Preaching*.
       N. Y., Henry Holt & Co., Inc., 1883.

1882-83   No lectures.

1883-84   Nathaniel Judson Burton, *In Pulpit and Parish:
       Yale Lectures on Preaching*, and other writings.
       Pilgrim Press, 1887. Reprinted by Macmillan
       Company, 1925.

1884-85   Henry Martyn Storrs, The American Preacher.
       Not published.

1885-86   William Mackergo Taylor, *The Scottish Pulpit*.
       N. Y., Harper & Brothers, 1887.

1886-87   Washington Gladden, *Tools and the Man*.
       Boston, Houghton Mifflin, 1893.

1887-88   Henry Clay Trumbull, *The Sunday School*.
       Philadelphia, John P. Wattles, 1888.

1888-89   John Albert Broadus, Preaching and the Ministerial
       Life.
       Not published.

1889-90   Adolphus Julius Frederick Behrends, *The Philos-
       ophy of Preaching*.
       N. Y., Charles Scribner's Sons, 1893.

1890-91   James Stalker, *The Preacher and His Models*.
       N. Y., A. C. Armstrong, 1893.

1891-92   Andrew Martin Fairbairn, *The Place of Christ in Modern Theology.*
N. Y., Charles Scribner's Sons, 1893.

1892-93   Robert Forman Horton, *Verbum Dei.*
N. Y., Macmillan Company, 1893.

1893-94   No lectures.

1894-95   David Hummell Greer, *The Preacher and His Place.*
N. Y., Charles Scribner's Sons, 1895.

1895-96   Henry van Dyke, *The Gospel for an Age of Doubt.*
N. Y., Macmillan Company, 1896.

1896-97   John Watson (Ian Maclaren), *The Cure of Souls.*
N. Y., Dodd & Mead, 1896.

1897-98   William Jewett Tucker, *The Making and Unmaking of the Preacher.*
Boston, Houghton Mifflin, 1898.

1898-99   Sir George Adam Smith, *Modern Criticism and the Preaching of the Old Testament.*
N. Y., A. C. Armstrong, 1901.

1899-00   John Brown, *Puritan Preaching in England.*
N. Y., Charles Scribner's Sons, 1900.

1900-01   No lectures.

1901-02   Washington Gladden, *Social Salvation.*
N. Y., Boston, Houghton Mifflin, 1902.

1902-03   George Angier Gordon, *Ultimate Conceptions of Faith.*
Boston, Houghton Mifflin, 1903.

1903-04 Lyman Abbott, *The Christian Ministry*.
Boston, Houghton Mifflin, 1905.

1904-05 Francis Greenwood Peabody, *Jesus Christ and the Christian Character*.
N. Y., Macmillan Company, 1908.

1905-06 Charles Reynolds Brown, *The Social Message of the Modern Pulpit*.
N. Y., Charles Scribner's Sons, 1906.

1906-07 Peter Taylor Forsyth, *Positive Preaching and the Modern Mind*.
London, Hodder & Stoughton, 1907.

1907-08 William Herbert Perry Faunce, *The Educational Ideal in the Ministry*.
N. Y., Macmillan Company, 1908; reprinted 1919.

1908-09 Herbert Hensley Henson, *The Liberty of Prophesying*.
New Haven, Yale University Press, 1910.

1909-10 Charles Edward Jefferson, *The Building of the Church*.
N. Y., Macmillan Company, 1910.

1910-11 Frank Wakeley Gunsaulus, *The Minister and the Spiritual Life*.
N. Y., Fleming M. Revell, 1911.

1911-12 John Henry Jowett, *The Preacher; His Life and Work*.
N. Y., George H. Doran, 1912.

1912-13 Charles Henry Parkhurst, *The Pulpit and the Pew*.
New Haven, Yale University Press, 1913.

1913-14   Charles Sylvester Horne, *The Romance of Preaching.*
N. Y., Fleming H. Revell, 1914.

1914-15   George Wharton Pepper, *A Voice from the Crowd.*
New Haven, Yale University Press, 1915.

1915-16   William DeWitt Hyde, *The Gospel of Good Will.*
N. Y., Macmillan Company, 1916.

1916-17   William Fraser McDowell, *Good Ministers of Jesus Christ.*
N. Y., Abingdon Press, 1917.

1917-18   Henry Sloane Coffin, *In a Day of Social Rebuilding.*
New Haven, Yale University Press, 1918.

1918-19   John Kelman, *The War and Preaching.*
New Haven, Yale University Press, 1919.

1919-20   Albert Parker Fitch, *Preaching and Paganism.*
New Haven, Yale University Press, 1920.

1920-21   Charles David Williams, *The Prophetic Ministry for Today.*
N. Y., Macmillan Company, 1921.

1921-22   William Pierson Merrill, *The Freedom of the Preacher.*
N. Y., Macmillan Company, 1922.

1922-23   Charles Reynolds Brown, *The Art of Preaching.*
N. Y., Macmillan Company, 1922.

1923-24   Harry Emerson Fosdick, *The Modern Use of the Bible.*
N. Y., Macmillan Company, 1924.

1924-25   William Ralph Inge, The Preaching of the Kingdom of God in Church History.
Not published.

1925-26   Raymond Calkins, *The Eloquence of the Christian
Experience.*
N. Y., Macmillan Company, 1927.

1926-27   John Robert Paterson Sclater, *The Public Worship
of God.*
N. Y., Doubleday, Doran, 1927.

1927-28   James Edward Freeman, *The Ambassador.*
N. Y., Macmillan Company, 1928.

1928-29   Edwin Du Bose Mouzon, *Preaching with Authority.*
N. Y., Doubleday, Doran, 1929.

1929-30   Francis John McConnell, *The Prophetic Ministry.*
N. Y., Abingdon Press, 1930.

1930-31   George Arthur Buttrick, *Jesus Came Preaching.*
N. Y., Charles Scribner's Sons, 1931.

1931-32   Ernest Fremont Tittle, *Jesus after Nineteen Centuries.*
N. Y., Abingdon Press, 1932.

1932-33   Lawrence Pearsall Jacks, *Elemental Religion.*
N. Y., Harper & Brothers, 1934.

1933-34   Albert Edward Day, *Jesus and Human Personality.*
N. Y., Abingdon Press, 1934.

1934-35   Walter Russell Bowie, *The Renewing Gospel.*
N. Y., Scribner's Sons, 1935.

1935-36   John Edgar Park, *The Miracle of Preaching.*
N. Y., Macmillan Company, 1936.

1936-37   No lectures.

1937-38   Willard Learoyd Sperry, *We Prophesy in Part.*
         N. Y., Harper & Brothers, 1938.

Index

Adler, 153
Alcott, Bronson, 150
Amos, 12, 15, 38-39, 138
Anabaptism, 77

Ben Sirach, 164
Berdyaev, 166-167
Bernard, Saint, 32
Bible, as literature, 53-56
Brooks, Phillips, 32-33, 69-70
Brothers Karamazov, 66

Calvin, 11, 37, 67
Carlyle, Thomas, 53
Cavell, Edith, 48-49
Ceremonial, and minister, 158-159
Chaucer, 164-165
Chesterton, 25
Choirilos of Samos, 164
Church in America, 84-85, 88-89; ministers of, 90-103
Coleman, Mr., 128
Coleridge, 68, 114
Congregationalism, 81-82
Cromwell, 23, 66
Cruelty, renascence of, 50-52

Damien, Father, 48
Denominationalism, 80

Eastern Orthodoxy. *See* Russian Church

Economics, and sermon, 36, 44-52
Eddington, 152
Edinburgh Review, 147
Einstein, 152
Emerson, 120
Emotion. *See* Feeling
Erotic symbolism, 25-26
Establishment, *vs.* Nonconformity
European situation today, 179-184
Ezekiel, 14, 42

Faith, *vs.* science, 146-147; nature of, 151
Fancy, *vs.* imagination, 147
Feeling, in sermon, 33, 34-35, 71
Ford Hall, Boston, 128-129
Freud, 153
Friends, Society of, 77, 189

Gandhi, 8
Garrison, William Lloyd, 47
Germany, Confessional Churches in, 173

Harnack, A. von, 62n., 89-90
Headlam, Dr. Arthur, 82
Heiler, 37
Henson, Rev. Hensley, 1n.
Hitler, 45
Hocking, Prof., 71

Human nature, and minister, 157-158

Imagination, *vs.* fancy, 147
Inspiration, 29-31, 34-35
Isaiah, 16

Jacks, Dr., 33, 114
James, William, 17
Jeans, 152
Jeremiah, 16, 26-27
Jesus, as a prophet, 38, 40-41, 56; ethical teachings of, 43-44
Judaism, disparagement of, 53
Jung, C. G., 111, 153

King, Henry Churchill, 5-6

Lake, Prof., 58
Landau, Rom, 130n.
Lenin, 8-9
Lincoln, Abraham, 15-16, 39, 48
Livingstone, 99
Luther, 11

Manchester Guardian, 157
Martyrs, early, 94-95
Marx, Karl, 9, 167
Masefield, John, 19
Meredith, George, 34, 137
Messianic prophecies, 39-41, 56-57
Minister, problems of, 134-157; necessary skills of, 157-163. *See also* Sermon, Church in America, etc.
Montanism, 77
Moore, George Foote, 29-30

Nathan, 38
Newman, Cardinal, 158
Nonconformity, *vs.* Establishment, 84

Oxford Group, 129-130

Park, J. Edgar, 142
Paul, Saint, 5, 57, 58, 59, 62-63, 72, 78, 102, 103, 107, 109, 112, 156
Peace, efforts for world, 170-174
Piers Plowman, 15
Pilgrims, 37
Pirké Aboth, 101
Politics, and sermon, 36, 44-52. *See also* Sermon, ideals of
Preaching, and minister, 159-163. *See also* Sermon
Priest, *vs.* prophet, 2, 82-83, 106
Prophecy, true origin of, 30; subjects for, 36-37; two major themes of, 38. *See also* Minister, Sermon, etc.
Prophet, *vs.* priest, 2, 82-83, 106; aim of true, 35; in Christian ministry, 78-79
Prophetic experience, nature of, 32
Prophets, the Hebrew, 7-8, 10-16, 25-27; and modern preachers, 29; *vs.* Christian, 58-64. *See also* Amos, Jeremiah, etc.
Protestantism, nature of, 3, 9; in America, 66; and Bible, 67-69; charges against, 187; future of, 188-189. *See also* Church in America

Quakers. *See* Friends, Society of

Reformation, Protestant, 11
Religion, perspective in, 185-189
Roman Church, 87, 89
Ropes, James Hardy, 9-10
Russian Church, 86-87, 89
Russian revolution, 167
Rutherford, Mark, 22

Sacraments, 104-105
Savonarola, 37
Schweitzer, 166
Science, *vs.* faith, 146-147
Sentimentality in sermon, 34, 71
Sermon, secret of, 29-31; emotion *vs.* sentimentality in, 33-34; modern problems and, 36, 44-52; American *vs.* Old World, 83-84, 149-150; modern, 104, 109-133; and New Testament, 106-109; ideals of, 175-185. *See also* Feeling, Sentimentality, Preaching, etc.
Shepard, Odell, 150

Skills, of minister, 157-163
Spengler, 168
Stalin, 45
Streeter, Canon, 17
Suicide, 170. *See also* Martyrs
Sunday Evening Forum Movement, 128-129
Survey, The, 49-50

Tauler, John, 33
Taylor, Jeremy, 1-2, 189-191
Theologia Germanica, 66
Thompson, Francis, 31
Thoreau, Henry, 125
Tolerance, 189-191
Tolstoi, Leo, 8, 15
Trevelyan, George Macaulay, 110, 161-162

Wells, H. G., 176
Whitehead, A. N., 44, 175
Wilson, Woodrow, 8, 173
Woolman, John, 52
Wordsworth, 12-13, 178
World Conference, on Faith and Order, 76, 121; on Life and Work, 121